# The Lady And The Nerd

## By Machell Proctor

ISBN: 9798304005234

# Table Of Contents

# Introduction

You know how some stories start with big, dramatic moments or lifelong dreams? Yeah, mine didn't. It all kicked off when I met this guy through my husband. He was a total nerd, if I'm being honest. Quiet, a little awkward, and way too into things like algorithms and data charts. On the surface, we couldn't have been more different. He and my husband started talking in what felt like a completely foreign language, and if you know me, you'll understand my initial reaction—a little defiance. Why? Because let's be real, that's how most of us are when new knowledge challenges us. It feels intimidating, and instead of leaning in, we shut the door and stay in our comfortable "system"—even when it hasn't produced real change.

But here's the thing: through months of casual fellowships, trips, and conversations, this man kept dropping little nuggets of knowledge that stirred up silent questions in me. He didn't push; he just shared. And then, after a while, I started listening. Really listening. And sure enough, that familiar friend—intimidation, mixed with pride—showed up. You know, that feeling where you don't want to ask questions because you're afraid of looking ignorant? But little by little, I let that go.

This nerd, David, as I came to know him, had a vast knowledge of numbers and financial systems that left me intrigued. He'd take me to new venues, introduce me to people having different conversations, and suddenly, I started seeing more—more for me, more for my family. He'd say things like, "Machell, you'd be an incredible asset to this industry," and I'd respond with, "Um, no sir. My brain doesn't work like yours. You're talking IUL, and all I know is IOU!" He'd just smile and keep pouring belief into me.

In the first six months of knowing him, he gave me about 20 books. Did I read them? Nope. Like many of us, I just put them on the shelf where they looked neat. But I kept hanging around, and one day, I heard someone in our circle speak in a way I could relate to. That's when my ears opened up completely, and I began to see the cracks in my own household.

We talk about legacy all the time, but until we answer these questions—what is it, what does it look like, and how do we achieve it—we're just rewriting the same chapters our ancestors did. That's when I realized the value of having a nerd in my life. David gave me an optical vision for my family's future. He helped me define a desired goal and craft a plan to achieve it.

The Bible says, "A wise woman builds her house, but a foolish one tears it down with her own hands." I didn't want to keep repeating habits that handed the enemy tools to destroy my household. I began to pray: "God, help me build a house. Clean my stained places, right my wrongs, and let my children walk in the promise of wisdom, knowledge, and understanding. Let them never see the sins of their forefathers repeated."

This journey isn't just about wealth; it's about transformation. It's about breaking generational curses and building a new foundation. As my husband often says, "On this path of life, you're never who you'll be when you reach your destiny. You're always becoming."

So, I embraced the process of becoming. I started listening, learning, and leaning into the tools I'd once been too intimidated to use. Now, I'm a woman who walks with a mindset of financial health and abundance. And as the Word says, "Now unto Him that is able…" Let's go! Welcome to The Lady and the Nerd.

# Chapter 1
# A Firm Financial Budget

## Understanding Financial Health

In 1998, I gave birth to my first child, a moment that profoundly reshaped my understanding of financial health. The realization hit me hard when David M. Walker, the CPA of the USA, articulated the dire financial trajectory of our nation. His warning wasn't just about national debt; it was a clarion call for every family to reevaluate their financial priorities. Financial health, I learned, is not merely about surviving but thriving and securing a stable future for our children.

The concept of financial health extends beyond the mere management of money. It involves making informed and strategic decisions that ensure both present stability and future security. As Walker highlighted, the mathematical inevitability of financial consequences can't be ignored. This understanding pushed me to delve deeper into the principles of budgeting, saving, and investing, which are crucial for safeguarding my family's future. It became clear that financial health is a continuous journey of learning and adapting.

Understanding financial health requires acknowledging the broader impact of our financial habits. The culture we raise our children in significantly shapes their perception of

3

money and success. Growing up, many of us were taught to view debt as a normal part of life, often glorified by the allure of credit cards and loans. However, financial health means breaking these cycles and instilling in our children the values of financial prudence and responsibility. It's about teaching them that true financial freedom comes from living within our means and avoiding unnecessary debt.

Financial health also involves emotional and psychological well-being. The stress and anxiety that come with financial instability can take a toll on our mental health. By understanding and managing our finances effectively, we can reduce this stress and create a more positive and stable environment for our families. This involves open and honest conversations about money, setting realistic expectations, and working together towards common financial goals. In this way, financial health contributes to overall family harmony and well-being.

In my journey, I found that financial health is closely tied to spiritual well-being. Scriptures like Romans 13:8, which advises us to owe nothing but love, and Psalms 37:21, which contrasts the wicked who borrow and do not repay with the righteous who are generous, offer profound insights into financial stewardship. These teachings emphasize the importance of integrity, generosity, and prudent financial management. By aligning our financial practices with these principles, we can achieve a sense of peace and fulfillment that transcends material wealth.

Lastly, financial health is about empowerment and legacy. It's about taking control of our financial destiny and creating a lasting legacy for our children. This involves not only managing our finances wisely but also educating and empowering our children to do the same. By fostering a culture of financial literacy and responsibility, we can ensure that future generations are better equipped to navigate the financial challenges of life. This legacy of financial health is one of the greatest gifts we can give to our children and grandchildren.

## Creating a Sustainable Budget

Creating a budget is the cornerstone of financial health, and it starts with understanding our financial landscape. Remember when David Walker sounded the alarm about the nation's fiscal health? It wasn't just a scare tactic—it was a wake-up call. It made me realize that to secure my family's future, I needed to get serious about budgeting. And let me tell you, budgeting isn't about living a life of restriction; it's about giving your money a purpose and making it work for you.

So, where do you start? First, you need to know where your money is going. Track your expenses for a month, and I mean every single dollar. You'll be surprised where your money goes—those daily coffees add up! Once you have a clear picture, categorize your expenses: housing, utilities, groceries, entertainment, etc. This is where the fun begins. You get to decide where your money goes. Prioritize needs over wants, but don't forget to allocate some for fun and leisure. A sustainable budget is balanced; it doesn't feel like punishment.

Setting a budget isn't a one-time event; it's a continuous process. Life happens, and your budget should be flexible enough to adapt. Unexpected expenses will come up—your car might need repairs, or you might have medical bills. This is where having an emergency fund is crucial. Aim to save at least three to six months' worth of expenses. It might sound daunting, but start small. Even $500 in an emergency fund can prevent a minor inconvenience from becoming a major financial setback.

Now, let's talk about savings. A good budget includes a savings plan. Pay yourself first by setting aside a portion of your income before you start spending. Automate your savings to make it easier. Whether it's saving for a rainy day, a vacation, or retirement, having specific goals makes saving more motivating. Visualize what you're saving for; it makes the process more rewarding. Imagine the peace of mind knowing you have a financial cushion or the joy of taking that dream vacation you've saved for.

Don't forget about debt management. High-interest debt, like credit card debt, can cripple your financial health. Focus on paying off high-interest debts first while making minimum payments on others. Use strategies like the snowball method (paying off the smallest debts first) or the avalanche method (tackling the highest interest rates first). Whichever method you choose, the key is consistency. Celebrate your progress, no matter how small. Every payment brings you one step closer to financial freedom.

Remember, a budget is a tool, not a rule. It's there to help you achieve your financial goals, not to make your life miserable. Review and adjust your budget regularly. Life changes—your budget should, too. And don't be afraid to seek help if you need it. Financial advisors, budgeting apps, and even books can offer guidance and support. The goal is to create a sustainable budget that fits your lifestyle and helps you build a secure financial future.

## Financial Goals

Setting financial goals is like mapping out a journey. Without a map, you might end up wandering aimlessly. Goals give you direction and purpose. They transform vague dreams into achievable milestones. When I first heard David Walker's warning, it struck me that I needed clear financial goals to navigate my family's future. And so, I began setting specific, measurable, achievable, relevant, and time-bound (SMART) financial goals.

First, let's get specific. What do you want to achieve? Do you want to buy a house, pay off debt, build an emergency fund, or save for retirement? Be as detailed as possible. For instance, instead of saying "I want to save money," say "I want to save $10,000 for a down payment on a house in two years." The more specific your goal, the easier it is to create a plan to achieve it.

Measurable goals help you track your progress and stay motivated. Break down big goals into smaller, manageable steps. If your goal is to save $10,000 in two years, that's about $417 per month. Knowing this monthly target makes the goal seem more attainable. Use tools like spreadsheets or budgeting apps to monitor your progress. Seeing those savings grow can be incredibly motivating.

Your goals should be achievable. Setting unrealistic goals sets you up for failure and frustration. Consider your current financial situation and any constraints you might have. It's okay to stretch yourself a little, but make sure your goals are within reach. For example, if saving $417 per month isn't feasible, adjust your timeline or find ways to cut expenses or increase your income.

Relevance is key. Your financial goals should align with your values and long-term plans. Think about why each goal is important to you. If your goal is to pay off debt, consider how it will improve your financial stability and peace of mind. If it's saving for a vacation, think about the joy and relaxation it will bring. Understanding the "why" behind your goals keeps you focused and committed.

Finally, set a timeline. Deadlines create a sense of urgency and help you stay on track. If your goal is open-ended, it's easy to procrastinate. Setting a clear timeline gives you a target to aim for and a way to measure your progress. Whether it's saving a certain amount by the end of the year or paying off a credit card in six months, having a timeline keeps you accountable.

## Debt Management

Debt can feel like a heavy chain around your neck, but it doesn't have to be a life sentence. The first step in managing debt is facing it head-on. List all your debts, including the interest rates and minimum payments. This can be a daunting task, but it's essential for creating a repayment plan. Knowledge is power, and understanding the full scope of your debt gives you control over it.

Next, prioritize your debts. High-interest debts, like credit cards, should be your primary focus because they cost you the most money over time. Consider using the avalanche method to tackle these first. Pay as much as you can towards the highest interest debt while making minimum payments on the rest. Once the highest interest debt is paid off, move to the next one. This method saves you money in the long run.

Alternatively, you might prefer the snowball method, which focuses on paying off the smallest debts first. This approach can be more psychologically rewarding, as it allows you to see quick progress. Paying off smaller debts can motivate you to keep going, building momentum as you move to larger debts. Choose the method that works best for you; the important thing is to stay consistent and committed.

Consider consolidating your debts to simplify your payments and potentially lower your interest rates. Balance transfer credit cards, personal loans, or home equity loans can consolidate multiple debts into one monthly payment. However, be cautious with this approach. Ensure you understand the terms and fees associated with debt consolidation, and avoid accruing new debt while paying off the consolidated loan.

Cutting expenses and increasing income are crucial steps in debt management. Review your budget to find areas where you can cut back. Can you reduce discretionary spending, such as dining out or subscription services? Can you negotiate lower bills or switch to cheaper alternatives? On the income side, consider taking on a side job or freelance work. Every extra dollar you earn can go towards paying off your debt faster.

Lastly, don't hesitate to seek professional help if you're overwhelmed. Credit counseling agencies can offer guidance and support, helping you create a debt management plan. They can negotiate with creditors on your behalf to lower interest rates or reduce monthly payments. Remember, managing debt is a journey, and it's okay to ask for help along the way. The goal is to regain control of your finances and move towards a debt-free future.

## Emergency Funds

Life is full of surprises, and not all of them are pleasant. That's why having an emergency fund is a game-changer. An emergency fund is your financial safety net, giving you peace of mind when the unexpected happens. Think of it as a buffer that protects you from life's curveballs—like sudden medical bills, car repairs, or even job loss. The goal is to have three to six months' worth of living expenses saved up. But don't let that number intimidate you; the key is to start small and build gradually.

Starting an emergency fund might seem daunting, especially if you're living paycheck to paycheck. But even setting aside a small amount each month can make a big difference. Begin with a modest goal—perhaps $500 to $1,000—and work your way up from there. Automate your savings so that a portion of your income goes directly into your emergency fund. This way, you're consistently saving without having to think about it.

The best place to keep your emergency fund is in a high-yield savings account. You want it to be easily accessible but separate from your everyday checking account to avoid the temptation to dip into it for non-emergencies. High-yield accounts offer better interest rates than regular savings accounts, allowing your money to grow a bit while it sits there. Remember, the primary purpose of an emergency fund is not to earn interest but to be readily available when you need it.

Having an emergency fund changes how you handle financial stress. Instead of panicking when an unexpected expense arises, you can calmly use your emergency fund to cover the cost. This reduces financial anxiety and allows you to focus on resolving the issue at hand. It also prevents you from resorting to high-interest debt, like credit cards, which can compound your financial problems. An emergency fund is an essential part of a healthy financial plan.

Let's talk about prioritizing your emergency fund. If you're also paying off debt, it might feel like a balancing act. Ideally, you should do both—allocate a portion of your income to debt repayment and a portion to your emergency fund. If you don't have any savings yet, focus on building a small emergency fund first, even if it's just $500. Once you have that cushion, you can shift more of your focus to paying off debt while continuing to build your savings.

An emergency fund is also about teaching your children financial responsibility. Involve them in the process and explain why it's important to save for the unexpected. Show them how you prioritize and manage your finances. This not only sets a good example but also prepares them for their own financial futures. Creating a habit of saving for emergencies can instill a sense of security and financial independence in the next generation.

# Understanding the Impact of Lifestyle Choices

Our lifestyle choices significantly impact our financial health, often in ways we don't immediately realize. The decisions we make daily—from the coffee we buy to the car we drive—shape our financial future. It's crucial to evaluate these choices and understand their long-term effects on our budget and financial goals. By making mindful decisions, we can improve our financial stability and overall well-being.

Consider the small, seemingly insignificant purchases we make regularly. That daily latte, while a delightful treat, adds up over time. If you're spending $5 a day on coffee, that's $150 a month or $1,800 a year! Imagine redirecting that money into your emergency fund or towards paying off debt. Small changes in our spending habits can lead to significant financial improvements without drastically altering our lifestyle.

Transportation is another area where lifestyle choices heavily impact finances. The allure of a brand-new car is strong, but so is the financial burden that comes with it. New cars depreciate quickly, and monthly payments can strain your budget. Opting for a reliable used car can save you thousands of dollars. Additionally, maintaining your vehicle properly can extend its life and save on costly repairs. It's about balancing desire with practicality and long-term benefits.

Housing is often our most significant expense, and our choices here can have a profound impact on our financial health. While it's tempting to buy the biggest house you can afford, it's essential to consider all associated costs—mortgage payments, property taxes, utilities, and maintenance. Living below your means in a more modest home can free up funds for savings and investments. It's about creating a comfortable, financially sustainable living situation rather than stretching your budget to its limit.

Entertainment and dining out are other areas where lifestyle choices affect our finances. While it's essential to enjoy life and treat ourselves, frequent dining out and entertainment expenses can quickly add up. Consider cooking more meals at home and finding free or low-cost entertainment options. It doesn't mean you have to give up fun; it's about finding a balance that allows you to enjoy life while still working towards your financial goals.

Finally, our health and wellness choices impact our finances. Investing in a healthy lifestyle can save you money in the long run by reducing medical expenses. Regular exercise, a balanced diet, and preventive healthcare can help you avoid costly health issues. Additionally, managing stress through healthy outlets can improve your overall quality of life and financial stability. It's a reminder that our bodies are our greatest assets, and taking care of them is a wise investment.

In conclusion, understanding the impact of our lifestyle choices on our finances is crucial for long-term financial health. By making mindful, informed decisions, we can align our spending with our financial goals, ensuring a stable and prosperous future. It's not about deprivation but about making choices that support a balanced, fulfilling life while securing our financial well-being.

# Financial Literacy for Kids

Teaching kids about money is one of the best investments we can make in their future. Financial literacy isn't typically taught in schools, so it's up to us as parents to fill that gap. By introducing financial concepts early, we can prepare our children to make smart financial decisions as they grow. It's about empowering them with knowledge and skills that will serve them throughout their lives.

Start with the basics. Introduce concepts like saving, spending, and earning in a way that's easy for them to understand. Use real-life examples and hands-on activities. For younger children, this might mean using a piggy bank to save for a toy. For older kids, consider opening a savings account and teaching them how to manage it. The key is to make learning about money fun and engaging.

Allowance is a great tool for teaching financial responsibility. It gives children hands-on experience with managing their own money. Set clear guidelines on how they can earn their allowance, whether through chores or other responsibilities. Encourage them to divide their money into categories: saving, spending, and giving. This teaches them the importance of budgeting and prioritizing their financial goals.

Introduce the concept of delayed gratification. In a world of instant gratification, it's essential for children to learn the value of waiting for things they want. Encourage them to save for larger purchases rather than spending their money immediately. This not only teaches patience but also the satisfaction that comes from achieving a financial goal. It's a lesson that will benefit them well into adulthood.

Use everyday experiences as teaching moments. Shopping trips, paying bills, or even discussing the family budget can be opportunities to teach your children about money. Explain why you make certain financial decisions and involve them in the process. For example, compare prices at the grocery store and discuss why you choose one product over another. These real-world examples make financial concepts tangible and understandable.

Finally, lead by example. Children learn by watching us. If we demonstrate good financial habits, they're likely to adopt them. Show them how you save, budget, and make thoughtful financial decisions. Be open about your financial goals and challenges. By modeling responsible financial behavior, you set a positive example for your children to follow.

Incorporating financial literacy into your children's upbringing equips them with the tools they need to manage their finances effectively. It's about laying a foundation that will support their future financial independence and success. Remember, the lessons you teach them today will shape their financial habits and attitudes for years to come.

# Chapter 2
# The Building of a Safe Legacy

## Defining Legacy

Legacy—it's a word that carries weight and significance. When you think about leaving a legacy, it's not just about material wealth but the values, wisdom, and traditions you pass down to future generations. For me, understanding legacy began with recognizing the impact of my actions and decisions on my children and their children. A legacy is built over time through intentional actions and thoughtful planning. It's about creating something enduring that benefits those who come after us.

Building a legacy starts with defining what you want to leave behind. What values do you want to instill in your children? What principles should guide their lives? For me, it was essential to teach my children the importance of faith, integrity, and financial responsibility. I wanted them to understand the value of hard work and the importance of giving back to the community. These are the building blocks of a meaningful legacy that extends beyond financial assets.

Financially, a legacy involves creating and preserving wealth that can be passed down. This means making smart investments, managing money wisely, and avoiding unnecessary debt. It's about ensuring that your children and grandchildren have the resources they need to pursue their dreams and live comfortably. But it's not just about giving them money; it's about equipping them with the knowledge and skills to manage it responsibly. Teaching financial literacy is a crucial part of building a lasting legacy.

Legacy also encompasses the emotional and spiritual inheritance you leave behind. The relationships you build, the love you share, and the guidance you provide shape your family's future. It's about creating memories, traditions, and values that your descendants will cherish and carry forward. For instance, sharing family stories, celebrating milestones together, and maintaining a close-knit family unit all contribute to a strong, enduring legacy. These intangible elements are often the most cherished aspects of what we leave behind.

In building a legacy, it's important to involve your family in the process. Discuss your goals and plans with them, and encourage them to share their own visions for the future. This fosters a sense of unity and shared purpose, ensuring that everyone is on the same page. It also helps your children understand the significance of their inheritance and prepares them to carry the legacy forward. By involving them, you also teach them the importance of planning and responsibility.

Finally, building a legacy requires consistent effort and commitment. It's not something that happens overnight; it's a lifelong endeavor. Regularly review and adjust your plans as needed, and stay focused on your long-term goals. Celebrate your achievements along the way and use setbacks as learning opportunities. Remember, a legacy is not just about what you leave behind, but the impact you make while you're here. It's about living a life that reflects your values and inspires those around you.

## Starting Early

When it comes to building a legacy, starting early is key. The earlier you begin, the more time you have to grow your wealth, instill values, and shape the future you envision for your family. I learned this lesson through my experiences and the stories of others who waited too long to start planning. Time is one of the most valuable assets in legacy building, and starting early allows you to harness its full potential.

One of the first steps in starting early is to set clear, achievable goals. What do you want to accomplish in the next five, ten, or twenty years? These goals will guide your actions and decisions. For example, if you want to ensure your children can attend college without financial strain, start a college savings plan as soon as they are born. The power of compound interest means that even small, regular contributions can grow significantly over time.

Investing early is another crucial aspect of building a legacy. The earlier you start investing, the more time your money has to grow. This doesn't mean you need to be an expert in the stock market. Start with basic, low-risk investments and gradually diversify as you become more comfortable. Real estate, retirement accounts, and education savings plans are excellent places to begin. The key is to start and let time work its magic.

Instilling values and principles in your children from a young age is equally important. Children absorb lessons from their surroundings, so create an environment that reflects the values you want them to embrace. Teach them about the importance of saving, giving, and spending wisely. Use everyday situations to impart these lessons. For instance, involve them in family budgeting or discuss the importance of charitable giving. These early lessons lay the foundation for responsible adulthood.

Starting early also means planning for the unexpected. Life is unpredictable, and having a plan in place can provide security and peace of mind. This includes having adequate insurance, creating a will, and considering trusts to protect your assets. It's also wise to have an emergency fund to cover unforeseen expenses. These measures ensure that your family is protected and your legacy is preserved, even in difficult times.

Involve your children in the legacy-building process from an early age. This not only prepares them for future responsibilities but also fosters a sense of ownership and pride in the family legacy. Share your goals and plans with them, and encourage them to ask questions and express their thoughts. This creates a family culture of openness and collaboration, which is essential for sustaining a legacy over generations.

Starting early is about taking proactive steps today to secure a better future for your family. It's about being intentional with your time, resources, and efforts. By starting now, you maximize the potential for growth and create a solid foundation for your legacy. Remember, the journey of a thousand miles begins with a single step. Take that step today and build the legacy you envision for your family.

## Family Involvement

Building a legacy is not a solo endeavor; it requires the active participation and commitment of the entire family. Family involvement is crucial for creating a legacy that is meaningful and sustainable. When everyone is on board, it fosters a sense of unity and purpose that strengthens the family bond. Involving your family in the legacy-building process ensures that your values and vision are carried forward by future generations.

Start by having open and honest conversations with your family about your legacy goals. Share your vision and explain why it's important to you. Encourage your family members to share their own ideas and aspirations. This creates a collaborative environment where everyone feels valued and heard. It's essential to ensure that the legacy reflects the collective values and goals of the family, not just the desires of one individual.

Regular family meetings can be an effective way to keep everyone informed and engaged. Use these meetings to discuss progress, address challenges, and celebrate achievements. Make them interactive and inclusive, allowing each family member to contribute. This not only keeps everyone aligned with the family's goals but also fosters a sense of ownership and responsibility. When everyone has a stake in the legacy, they are more likely to work towards its success.

Education is a key component of family involvement. Equip your family with the knowledge and skills they need to manage and grow the legacy. This includes financial literacy, investment strategies, and estate planning. Consider bringing in experts to provide training or attending workshops together as a family. The more knowledgeable your family is, the better equipped they will be to preserve and enhance the legacy. Education empowers your family to make informed decisions and take proactive steps towards achieving the legacy goals.

Encourage family members to take on roles and responsibilities that align with their strengths and interests. This not only distributes the workload but also ensures that everyone is contributing in a meaningful way. For example, one family member might manage the finances, while another focuses on community involvement or family traditions. By leveraging each person's unique skills and passions, you create a well-rounded and dynamic approach to building the legacy.

Involve the younger generation early on. Teach children about the family's legacy and the importance of their role in it. Use age-appropriate activities to instill values and principles. For instance, you might involve them in charitable activities, teach them about saving and budgeting, or share stories about the family's history and achievements. By engaging them from a young age, you nurture a sense of pride and responsibility that will carry forward as they grow older.

Finally, make the legacy-building process enjoyable and rewarding. Celebrate milestones and successes, no matter how small. Recognize and appreciate each family member's contributions. This creates positive reinforcement and keeps everyone motivated. Remember, building a legacy is a journey, not a destination. By involving your family and making it a shared endeavor, you create a lasting legacy that is rich in values, wisdom, and unity.

## Educational Investments

Investing in education is one of the most impactful ways to build a legacy that lasts. Education opens doors to opportunities, fosters personal growth, and equips individuals with the skills they need to succeed. For my family, ensuring that my children have access to quality education has always been a top priority. Education is not just about academic knowledge; it's about cultivating curiosity, critical thinking, and a lifelong love of learning.

One of the first steps in investing in education is to start early. From a young age, expose your children to a variety of learning experiences. Encourage reading, exploration, and curiosity. Provide them with books, educational toys, and opportunities to learn new skills. Early education lays the foundation for future academic success and instills a love of learning that will serve them throughout their lives.

Consider the long-term benefits of higher education. College and university degrees can open doors to better job opportunities and higher earning potential. However, the cost of higher education can be daunting. Start saving early by setting up education savings plans, such as 529 plans or custodial accounts. These accounts offer tax advantages and can grow significantly over time. Even small, regular contributions can make a big difference when it comes time for your children to attend college.

Encourage your children to pursue their passions and interests. Education is most effective when it aligns with an individual's strengths and passions. Whether your child is interested in the arts, sciences, or trades, support their interests and help them explore potential career paths. This might involve extracurricular activities, specialized programs, or internships. By nurturing their passions, you help them find fulfilling careers and contribute meaningfully to their legacy.

Financial literacy is an essential part of educational investments. Teach your children about money management, budgeting, and investing. These skills are crucial for their financial independence and success. Consider involving them in family financial discussions and decisions. This not only provides practical knowledge but also helps them understand the value of money and the importance of making informed financial choices.

Beyond formal education, consider the value of lifelong learning. Encourage your family to continue learning and growing throughout their lives. This might involve professional development courses, workshops, or self-study. Lifelong learning keeps the mind sharp, fosters innovation, and helps individuals adapt to changing circumstances. By promoting a culture of continuous learning, you ensure that your legacy evolves and thrives in an ever-changing world.

## Long-Term Planning

Long-term planning is essential for building a legacy that endures through generations. It's about looking ahead, anticipating challenges, and making informed decisions that ensure the stability and growth of your family's wealth and values. Long-term planning involves a combination of financial strategies, estate planning, and ongoing education. It's a continuous process that requires dedication and foresight.

One of the most critical aspects of long-term planning is estate planning. This involves creating a will, setting up trusts, and making arrangements for the distribution of your assets. A well-crafted estate plan ensures that your wealth is passed down according to your wishes and can minimize taxes and legal complications. Consider working with a financial advisor or estate planner to create a comprehensive plan that protects your assets and provides for your family.

Investing for the long term is another crucial element of building a legacy. This means diversifying your investments to spread risk and maximize returns over time. Consider a mix of stocks, bonds, real estate, and other assets that align with your risk tolerance and financial goals. Regularly review and adjust your investment portfolio to ensure it remains aligned with your long-term objectives. The power of compound interest means that the earlier you start investing, the greater the potential for growth.

Long-term planning also involves preparing for potential challenges and uncertainties. This includes having adequate insurance coverage to protect against unforeseen events, such as illness, disability, or death. Life insurance, health insurance, and disability insurance are essential components of a robust long-term plan. These measures provide financial security for your family and ensure that your legacy is protected in the face of adversity.

Educating your family about the importance of long-term planning is crucial. Share your plans and goals with them, and involve them in the process. This fosters a sense of responsibility and ensures that they are prepared to carry on your legacy. Consider setting up family meetings to discuss financial goals, review progress, and make any necessary adjustments. Transparency and communication are key to successful long-term planning.

Finally, remember that long-term planning is not a one-time event but an ongoing process. Regularly review and update your plans to reflect changes in your circumstances, goals, and the financial landscape. Stay informed about new opportunities and potential risks. By remaining proactive and adaptable, you can ensure that your legacy continues to grow and thrive for generations to come.

## Protecting Your Legacy

Protecting your legacy involves taking proactive steps to safeguard your wealth, values, and family's future. This requires a combination of legal measures, financial strategies, and continuous education. The goal is to ensure that your legacy remains intact and can be passed down to future generations without unnecessary complications or losses.

One of the first steps in protecting your legacy is to establish clear legal protections. This includes creating a comprehensive estate plan with a will, trusts, and power of attorney. A will outlines your wishes for the distribution of your assets, while trusts can provide more detailed control and protection of those assets. Power of attorney ensures that someone you trust can make decisions on your behalf if you are unable to do so. These legal documents are essential for avoiding probate, reducing taxes, and ensuring that your wishes are honored.

Insurance is another critical component of protecting your legacy. Life insurance provides financial support for your family in the event of your death, ensuring that they can maintain their standard of living and cover expenses such as mortgages, education, and everyday living costs. Health and disability insurance protect against the financial impact of illness or injury, allowing you to focus on recovery without the added stress of financial strain. Adequate insurance coverage is a fundamental part of a robust legacy protection plan.

Diversifying your investments is a key strategy for minimizing risk and protecting your wealth. By spreading your investments across different asset classes, such as stocks, bonds, real estate, and commodities, you reduce the impact of market volatility on your overall portfolio. Regularly review and adjust your investments to align with your risk tolerance and financial goals. A well-diversified portfolio is more resilient to economic fluctuations and can better withstand financial challenges.

Educating your family about financial literacy and the importance of protecting the legacy is crucial. Share your financial plans and strategies with them, and involve them in decision-making processes. This not only prepares them to manage and grow the legacy but also fosters a sense of responsibility and stewardship. Consider holding regular family meetings to discuss financial goals, review progress, and address any concerns. Education and communication are key to ensuring that your family is well-equipped to protect and carry forward the legacy.

Protecting your legacy also means being vigilant about potential threats and taking steps to mitigate them. This includes staying informed about changes in tax laws, market conditions, and other factors that could impact your financial plans. Work with financial advisors, estate planners, and other professionals to stay up-to-date and make informed decisions. Regularly review and update your legal and financial documents to reflect any changes in your circumstances or goals.

Finally, consider the emotional and relational aspects of protecting your legacy. Building strong, healthy relationships within your family is essential for ensuring that your legacy endures. Encourage open communication, resolve conflicts constructively, and foster a sense of unity and shared purpose. A strong family bond provides a solid foundation for protecting and sustaining your legacy through generations.

# Chapter 3
# Development of Generational Wealth

## Wealth vs. Income

Let's get real—understanding the difference between wealth and income is a game-changer. Income is what you earn; wealth is what you keep and grow. Many people make the mistake of focusing solely on earning more money, thinking that will solve all their problems. But true financial freedom comes from building wealth, not just earning a high income. It's like the difference between running on a hamster wheel and planting a tree that bears fruit year after year.

Think of income as the seeds you plant and wealth as the tree that grows. You can earn a fantastic salary, but if you spend it all, you're left with nothing. Wealth, on the other hand, is about accumulating assets that generate more income over time. It's about making your money work for you. Picture this: instead of just earning a paycheck, you're building a portfolio of investments, real estate, and businesses that provide passive income. This is the essence of generational wealth.

Building wealth starts with a mindset shift. You need to change how you view money and financial success. It's not about immediate gratification but long-term benefits. Start by tracking your net worth—the total value of your assets minus your liabilities. This gives you a clear picture of your financial health and helps you set realistic goals. Celebrate each milestone as your net worth grows, and use it as motivation to keep going.

Investing is a crucial component of wealth building. Don't let the idea of investing intimidate you. Start small and gradually increase your investments as you become more comfortable. Diversify your portfolio to spread risk and maximize returns. Consider stocks, bonds, mutual funds, and real estate. Remember, investing is a marathon, not a sprint. The power of compound interest means that even small investments can grow significantly over time.

Living below your means is another key strategy. Just because you earn a lot doesn't mean you have to spend a lot. Adopt a frugal mindset and prioritize saving and investing over spending. This doesn't mean you have to deprive yourself of life's pleasures, but rather make conscious choices about where your money goes. For example, instead of buying the latest gadget, invest that money in a stock or a savings account. Over time, these small sacrifices will pay off in a big way.

Lastly, educate yourself continuously. The financial world is always changing, and staying informed is crucial. Read books, attend seminars, and follow financial news. The more you know, the better equipped you'll be to make smart financial decisions. Remember, building wealth is a journey, not a destination. Stay committed, stay informed, and watch your wealth grow.

## Investing Wisely

Alright, let's dive into the exciting world of investing! Investing wisely is the secret sauce to building generational wealth. It's like planting a garden—you sow seeds, nurture them, and watch them grow into a bountiful harvest. But here's the thing: you don't need to be a financial wizard to start investing. You just need a willingness to learn and a bit of patience.

First things first, understand your risk tolerance. Are you a thrill-seeker who enjoys high-stakes, high-reward opportunities, or do you prefer playing it safe with steady, reliable returns? Knowing your risk tolerance helps you choose the right investments. For beginners, it's often wise to start with low-risk investments and gradually diversify into higher-risk options as you gain confidence and experience.

Diversification is your best friend. Imagine you're at a buffet—you wouldn't fill your plate with just one dish, right? The same principle applies to investing. Spread your money across different asset classes: stocks, bonds, real estate, and mutual funds. This reduces risk because if one investment underperforms, others may perform well, balancing out your portfolio. Think of it as a safety net that protects your wealth.

Start with index funds if you're a newbie. Index funds are like a pre-packed meal—they contain a mix of various stocks or bonds, offering instant diversification. They're low-cost, easy to manage, and have historically provided solid returns. Over time, you can explore other options like individual stocks, real estate, or even venture into more specialized investments like cryptocurrency or precious metals.

Now, let's talk about the power of compound interest. Albert Einstein called it the eighth wonder of the world, and for good reason. Compound interest means you earn interest on your initial investment, plus on the interest that accumulates over time. It's like a snowball rolling down a hill, gaining size and speed. The earlier you start investing, the more you benefit from compounding. Even small investments can grow substantially over decades.

Regularly review and adjust your investment portfolio. The financial market is dynamic, and so are your life circumstances. Set a schedule to review your investments—quarterly or annually works well for most people. Assess your performance, re-balance your portfolio if necessary, and make sure your investments align with your financial goals and risk tolerance. This proactive approach keeps your investments on track and maximizes your returns.

Finally, educate yourself and seek professional advice if needed. There are countless resources available—books, podcasts, online courses, and financial advisors. Don't be afraid to ask questions and learn from experts. Investing can seem daunting at first, but with knowledge and practice, you'll become more confident and savvy. Remember, every investor starts somewhere, and the key is to start. The sooner you begin, the sooner you can start building wealth.

## Entrepreneurship

Entrepreneurship is one of the most powerful pathways to generational wealth. It's about taking control of your financial destiny, creating something from nothing, and reaping the rewards of your hard work and innovation. Starting your own business might seem intimidating, but with the right mindset and strategies, it can be incredibly rewarding. Let's explore how you can harness the power of entrepreneurship to build lasting wealth.

First, identify your passion and strengths. What are you good at? What do you love doing? Your business should be built around something you're passionate about and skilled at. This ensures that you stay motivated and enjoy the journey. Remember, passion drives perseverance, and perseverance is key to overcoming the inevitable challenges of entrepreneurship. Reflect on your experiences, talents, and interests, and find a niche where you can excel and make a difference.

Next, create a solid business plan. A well-thought-out business plan is your roadmap to success. It outlines your business goals, target market, competitive landscape, marketing strategy, and financial projections. Think of it as a blueprint that guides your actions and decisions. A detailed business plan not only helps you stay focused and organized but also attracts investors and partners who believe in your vision.

Networking is essential in the entrepreneurial world. Surround yourself with like-minded individuals who inspire and support you. Attend industry events, join professional associations, and engage in online communities. Building a strong network opens doors to new opportunities, provides valuable insights, and offers a support system when you face challenges. Remember, it's not just what you know, but who you know that can make a significant difference in your entrepreneurial journey.

Embrace failure as a learning opportunity. Every successful entrepreneur has faced setbacks and failures. The key is to learn from these experiences and keep moving forward. View failures as valuable lessons that teach you what works and what doesn't. This resilience and adaptability are crucial traits for any entrepreneur. Celebrate your successes, but also take the time to analyze and grow from your failures. They are stepping stones to your ultimate success.

Stay financially savvy. Managing your finances effectively is critical for business success. Keep a close eye on your cash flow, maintain a budget, and plan for taxes. Invest in accounting software or hire a professional accountant to ensure your financial records are accurate and up-to-date. Understanding your financial health allows you to make informed decisions, attract investors, and ensure the long-term sustainability of your business.

Finally, give back to your community. Successful entrepreneurship is not just about personal gain but also about making a positive impact on others. Engage in corporate social responsibility initiatives, support local charities, and create job opportunities in your community. Giving back not only enhances your brand's reputation but also creates a sense of fulfillment and purpose. Building a business that contributes to the greater good is a powerful way to create a lasting legacy.

Embrace the entrepreneurial journey with enthusiasm and determination. It's a challenging path, but the rewards—both financial and personal—are well worth it. By following these principles and staying committed to your vision, you can build a thriving business that generates wealth for you and your family for generations to come.

# Real Estate

Real estate is a cornerstone of generational wealth. It's tangible, has intrinsic value, and can provide steady income and long-term appreciation. When I first considered investing in real estate, I was overwhelmed by the complexities. But once I understood the basics and saw the potential returns, I realized that real estate could be a powerful tool for building and preserving wealth. Let's dive into how you can leverage real estate to secure your family's financial future.

The first step in real estate investing is education. Understand the market, the different types of properties, and the factors that affect property values. Read books, take courses, and seek advice from experienced investors. Knowledge is power, and the more you know, the better decisions you'll make. Don't rush into your first investment. Take the time to understand the ins and outs of real estate to mitigate risks and maximize returns.

Location, location, location! It's a cliché, but it's true—location is everything in real estate. Properties in desirable areas tend to appreciate more over time and attract higher rents. Look for locations with strong job markets, good schools, and amenities like parks and shopping centers. Research future development plans in the area, as they can significantly impact property values. Investing in the right location can make all the difference in the success of your real estate venture.

Start small and scale up. If you're new to real estate, consider starting with a single-family rental property. It's simpler to manage and a great way to learn the ropes. Once you're comfortable, you can diversify into multifamily properties, commercial real estate, or even real estate investment trusts (REITs). Each type of property has its own set of challenges and rewards, so diversify to spread risk and increase potential returns.

Financing is a critical aspect of real estate investing. Understand your financing options and choose the one that best suits your situation. Conventional mortgages, FHA loans, and private lending are just a few of the options available. Shop around for the best rates and terms. Remember, the goal is to maximize your return on investment, so minimizing your financing costs is crucial. Work with a mortgage broker or financial advisor if you need guidance.

Manage your properties effectively to ensure steady income and property appreciation. This involves regular maintenance, tenant management, and staying compliant with local laws and regulations. Consider hiring a property management company if you don't have the time or expertise to manage the properties yourself. A good property manager can handle the day-to-day operations, allowing you to focus on growing your portfolio.

Finally, think long-term. Real estate is not a get-rich-quick scheme; it's a long-term investment that requires patience and commitment. Hold onto properties for as long as possible to benefit from appreciation and rental income. Regularly review your portfolio and make adjustments as needed. Reinvest profits into new properties to continue building your wealth. By taking a long-term approach, you can create a real estate portfolio that provides financial security for generations.

## Financial Education

Financial education is the foundation of generational wealth. It's not just about knowing how to save or invest; it's about understanding the principles that govern money and how to make informed decisions. When I started my financial journey, I realized that knowledge was my most powerful tool. By educating yourself and your family about finances, you can make smarter choices, avoid common pitfalls, and build a legacy of financial literacy and independence.

Start with the basics. Financial education begins with understanding fundamental concepts like budgeting, saving, investing, and debt management. Teach your children these basics from a young age. Use practical, everyday situations to illustrate these concepts. For example, involve them in grocery shopping and show them how to compare prices and make a budget. These simple lessons lay the groundwork for more advanced financial knowledge.

Invest in your financial education continuously. The financial world is constantly evolving, and staying informed is crucial. Read books, attend seminars, follow financial news, and take online courses. There are countless resources available, from beginner guides to advanced investment strategies. The more you learn, the more confident and capable you'll become in managing your finances. Make financial education a lifelong pursuit for yourself and your family.

Teach critical thinking and decision-making skills. Financial education is not just about learning facts; it's about developing the ability to analyze situations and make informed decisions. Encourage your family to ask questions, seek out information, and consider different perspectives. When faced with financial decisions, weigh the pros and cons, assess the risks and rewards, and make thoughtful, informed choices. These skills are invaluable in navigating the complexities of the financial world.

Use technology to your advantage. There are many apps and tools available that can help you manage your finances, track your spending, and invest wisely. Introduce these tools to your family and show them how to use them effectively. Budgeting apps, investment platforms, and financial planning tools can simplify the process and provide valuable insights. Embrace technology to enhance your financial education and make managing money more accessible and efficient.

Promote open discussions about money. Many families avoid talking about finances, which can lead to misunderstandings and poor financial habits. Foster an environment where financial discussions are welcomed and encouraged. Share your financial goals, successes, and challenges with your family. This transparency helps build trust and ensures that everyone is on the same page. It also allows you to pass on your knowledge and experiences to the next generation.

Lead by example. Your actions speak louder than words. Demonstrate good financial habits in your daily life. Show your family how you budget, save, invest, and make financial decisions. Your behavior sets the standard for your children and teaches them the importance of financial responsibility. By modeling smart financial practices, you instill these values in your family and set the stage for a legacy of financial literacy and success.

## Financial Independence

Financial independence is the ultimate goal of building generational wealth. It's the freedom to live life on your own terms, without being constrained by financial worries. Achieving financial independence requires discipline, planning, and a long-term perspective. But the rewards are immense—imagine waking up each day knowing that you have the resources to pursue your passions, support your family, and enjoy life to the fullest.

Start by defining what financial independence means to you. For some, it might mean having enough savings to retire comfortably. For others, it could be the ability to work part-time or pursue a passion project without worrying about money. Clearly define your goals and create a plan to achieve them. Having a clear vision of your financial independence helps you stay focused and motivated on your journey.

Build multiple streams of income. Relying on a single source of income can be risky. Diversify your income sources to create a more stable financial foundation. This might include a combination of salary, rental income, dividends, interest from savings, and business income. Multiple income streams not only increase your financial security but also accelerate your path to financial independence. Look for opportunities to create passive income, which requires less ongoing effort but provides continuous returns.

Prioritize saving and investing. The more you save and invest, the faster you'll reach financial independence. Aim to save a significant portion of your income—experts often recommend at least 20%. Invest these savings wisely to grow your wealth over time. Use tax-advantaged accounts like 401(k)s and IRAs to maximize your savings and take advantage of employer matching programs if available. The power of compound interest can significantly boost your savings and help you achieve your goals faster.

Live below your means. One of the most effective ways to build wealth is to spend less than you earn. This requires a mindset shift from consumption to conservation. Evaluate your expenses and find areas where you can cut back without sacrificing your quality of life. Redirect these savings into investments and watch your wealth grow. Remember, financial independence is about having the freedom to make choices, not about living a life of deprivation.

Protect your wealth with insurance and estate planning. Ensure that you have adequate insurance coverage to protect against unexpected events, such as illness, disability, or death. This includes health insurance, life insurance, and disability insurance. Additionally, create an estate plan to ensure that your assets are distributed according to your wishes and to minimize taxes and legal complications. Proper protection of your wealth is essential for maintaining financial independence.

Finally, maintain a long-term perspective. Achieving financial independence is a marathon, not a sprint. Stay disciplined, be patient, and keep your focus on your long-term goals. Regularly review your progress and make adjustments as needed. Celebrate your milestones along the way and keep moving forward. By staying committed to your plan, you can achieve financial independence and create a legacy of freedom and prosperity for future generations.

# Chapter 4
# The Protection of the Legacy

## Legal Protection

When it comes to protecting your legacy, legal protection is your first line of defense. Imagine building a beautiful sandcastle on the beach only to watch the tide wash it away. Without proper legal safeguards, the wealth and legacy you've built could be eroded by taxes, legal battles, or mismanagement. Establishing solid legal protection ensures that your hard-earned assets are preserved and passed down according to your wishes.

The foundation of legal protection is a comprehensive estate plan. This plan includes key documents such as a will, trusts, power of attorney, and healthcare directives. A will specifies how your assets should be distributed after your death. It's crucial to keep this document up to date, reflecting any changes in your family situation or financial status. Trusts, on the other hand, can provide more control over the distribution of your assets, protect against estate taxes, and avoid the lengthy probate process. Consult an estate planning attorney to create a plan tailored to your unique needs and goals.

Trusts are particularly powerful tools in estate planning. They allow you to set specific conditions for how and when your assets are distributed. For example, you can establish a trust that provides for your children's education or stipulates that funds be distributed only when they reach a certain age. This control ensures that your legacy supports your family in the way you intend. Additionally, certain types of trusts, like irrevocable trusts, can protect your assets from creditors and lawsuits, further safeguarding your legacy.

Power of attorney and healthcare directives are also essential components of legal protection. A power of attorney allows a trusted person to make financial and legal decisions on your behalf if you become incapacitated. Similarly, healthcare directives outline your medical preferences and designate someone to make healthcare decisions for you. These documents ensure that your wishes are respected and prevent legal disputes that could drain your resources and disrupt your family.

Regularly review and update your estate plan to ensure it reflects your current situation and goals. Life changes, such as marriage, divorce, the birth of a child, or significant financial changes, should prompt a review of your estate plan. Additionally, changes in laws and regulations can impact your estate planning strategies. Staying proactive and keeping your plan current is crucial for maintaining the integrity of your legacy.

Finally, educate your family about your estate plan and the importance of legal protection. Open communication helps prevent misunderstandings and conflicts. Discuss your plans with your loved ones and explain your decisions. This transparency fosters trust and ensures that your family is prepared to manage and protect your legacy according to your wishes. By taking these legal steps, you can ensure that your legacy is preserved and passed down smoothly to future generations.

# Insurance

Insurance is a critical component of protecting your legacy. It acts as a financial safety net, safeguarding your wealth and ensuring that your family is taken care of in the face of unexpected events. Think of insurance as a fortress around your assets, providing a buffer against life's uncertainties. By having the right insurance coverage, you can protect your legacy from potential financial setbacks and provide peace of mind for you and your loved ones.

Life insurance is one of the most important types of insurance for legacy protection. It provides a financial cushion for your family in the event of your death, ensuring that they can maintain their standard of living and cover essential expenses. Life insurance proceeds can be used to pay off debts, cover funeral costs, and provide ongoing income for your family. There are different types of life insurance policies—term life, whole life, and universal life—each with its own benefits and considerations. Choose a policy that aligns with your financial goals and family needs.

Health insurance is another essential form of protection. Medical expenses can quickly deplete your savings and impact your financial stability. Having comprehensive health insurance coverage ensures that you and your family have access to necessary medical care without the burden of exorbitant costs. Additionally, consider long-term care insurance, which covers the costs of long-term care services, such as nursing home care or in-home care. This type of insurance can protect your assets from being drained by long-term care expenses and provide quality care for you or your loved ones.

Disability insurance is crucial for protecting your income if you become unable to work due to illness or injury. This type of insurance provides a portion of your salary, allowing you to cover living expenses and maintain your financial obligations. Disability insurance ensures that you can continue to support your family and protect your assets even if you are unable to work. It's an essential safeguard for anyone who relies on their income to maintain their lifestyle and build their legacy.

Property and casualty insurance protect your physical assets, such as your home, car, and personal belongings. Homeowners or renters insurance covers damage or loss due to events like fire, theft, or natural disasters. Auto insurance provides coverage for accidents, theft, and other damages to your vehicle. These policies ensure that you can repair or replace your property without incurring significant out-of-pocket expenses. Maintaining adequate property and casualty insurance is essential for protecting the physical components of your legacy.

Umbrella insurance provides additional liability coverage beyond the limits of your standard policies. This type of insurance is particularly valuable if you have significant assets or are at risk of being sued. Umbrella insurance covers a wide range of scenarios, including personal injury claims, property damage, and certain legal fees. It acts as an extra layer of protection, ensuring that your assets are shielded from major financial liabilities.

In summary, insurance is a vital tool for protecting your legacy from financial risks and uncertainties. By having the right coverage in place, you can ensure that your family is protected, your assets are secure, and your legacy remains intact. Regularly review your insurance policies and adjust coverage as needed to align with your changing needs and financial goals. With comprehensive insurance protection, you can build and preserve a lasting legacy for future generations.

## Asset Protection

Asset protection is all about safeguarding your wealth from potential threats, ensuring that what you've worked hard to build remains secure. It's like fortifying a castle—just as you'd protect a physical fortress from invaders, you need to protect your financial fortress from lawsuits, creditors, and other risks. Effective asset protection strategies can shield your wealth and provide peace of mind, knowing that your legacy is safe.

One of the first steps in asset protection is structuring your assets in a way that minimizes risk. This often involves the use of legal entities such as trusts, limited liability companies (LLCs), and corporations. These structures can separate your personal assets from your business or investment assets, reducing your exposure to liability. For instance, holding real estate properties in an LLC can protect your personal assets from claims related to those properties. Consult with an attorney to determine the best structure for your assets based on your specific circumstances.

Trusts are powerful tools for asset protection. An irrevocable trust, in particular, can provide significant protection because the assets placed in the trust are no longer considered your personal property. This means they are generally shielded from creditors and legal claims. Additionally, trusts can offer privacy, as they are not typically subject to public record like a will. By placing your assets in a trust, you can protect your wealth while also ensuring that it is managed and distributed according to your wishes.

Another key strategy is liability insurance. While we discussed the importance of various types of insurance earlier, liability insurance specifically protects you from claims and lawsuits. This can include general liability insurance, professional liability insurance, and personal umbrella policies. Liability insurance acts as a financial buffer, covering legal fees, settlements, and judgments. It's an essential layer of protection, especially if you have substantial assets or operate in a high-risk profession.

Maintaining a diverse portfolio can also protect your assets. Diversification spreads risk across different types of investments and asset classes, reducing the impact of any single loss. This means not putting all your eggs in one basket. Invest in a mix of stocks, bonds, real estate, and other assets. Diversification not only helps in growing your wealth but also in protecting it from market volatility and economic downturns.

Proactive financial management is critical for asset protection. This involves regularly reviewing your financial situation, staying informed about changes in laws and regulations, and making adjustments as needed. Work with financial advisors, accountants, and attorneys who specialize in asset protection. They can help you develop and implement strategies that align with your goals and provide ongoing support to ensure your assets remain protected.

Finally, plan for the unexpected. Life is full of uncertainties, and having contingency plans in place can protect your assets in the face of unforeseen events. This might include setting up emergency funds, creating succession plans for your business, and ensuring that your estate plan is current. By planning for the unexpected, you can minimize the impact of crises and ensure that your legacy remains secure.

In conclusion, asset protection is a multifaceted approach to securing your wealth and ensuring the longevity of your legacy. By structuring your assets wisely, utilizing trusts, obtaining adequate insurance, diversifying your portfolio, managing your finances proactively, and planning for contingencies, you can build a robust defense against potential threats. Protecting your assets is not just about safeguarding your wealth but also about preserving the legacy you've worked hard to create for future generations.

## Trusts and Estates

Trusts and estates are like the secret weapons in your financial arsenal. They offer control, protection, and efficiency in managing and distributing your wealth. Think of trusts as the Swiss Army knife of estate planning—they can do so many things! Trusts and estates not only help you avoid probate but also provide a clear roadmap for your heirs, ensuring that your legacy is handled exactly as you envision.

Let's start with the basics. A trust is a legal arrangement where one party, known as the trustee, holds and manages assets on behalf of another party, the beneficiary. There are many types of trusts, each serving different purposes. Revocable trusts, also known as living trusts, allow you to retain control over the assets during your lifetime and make changes as needed. Irrevocable trusts, once established, cannot be altered and offer stronger protection against creditors and estate taxes.

Why are trusts so powerful? For one, they bypass the probate process, which can be time-consuming, expensive, and public. With a trust, your assets can be distributed to your beneficiaries quickly and privately. This is particularly beneficial if you have complex assets or wish to keep the details of your estate confidential. Trusts also allow for more detailed and specific instructions on how your assets should be managed and distributed, providing you with peace of mind.

Estate planning goes hand in hand with trusts. Your estate plan is a comprehensive strategy that outlines how your assets will be managed and distributed after your death. This includes creating a will, setting up trusts, and designating beneficiaries for your retirement accounts and life insurance policies. A well-crafted estate plan ensures that your wishes are honored, your loved ones are provided for, and your estate is distributed efficiently.

When setting up a trust, choose a reliable trustee. This can be a family member, a trusted friend, or a professional fiduciary. The trustee is responsible for managing the trust assets according to your instructions, so it's crucial to select someone who is trustworthy and capable. You can also appoint a successor trustee to take over if the original trustee is unable to fulfill their duties. This ensures continuity and stability in the management of your trust.

Consider special types of trusts for specific needs. For example, a charitable trust allows you to support your favorite causes while providing tax benefits. A special needs trust ensures that a disabled beneficiary receives care and support without jeopardizing their eligibility for government benefits. Education trusts can be established to fund your children's or grandchildren's education. Tailor your trusts to meet the unique needs of your family and legacy.

Regularly review and update your trusts and estate plan. Life changes—such as marriages, divorces, births, and deaths—can impact your estate planning needs. Keep your plan current to reflect your evolving circumstances and goals. Work with an estate planning attorney to ensure that your documents are legally sound and aligned with your intentions. By staying proactive, you can ensure that your legacy is protected and preserved for future generations.

## Financial Advisors

Navigating the complexities of wealth management and legacy planning can be daunting, but you don't have to do it alone. Financial advisors are like seasoned guides who can help you chart a course through the financial landscape. They bring expertise, experience, and an objective perspective, helping you make informed decisions and avoid common pitfalls. Engaging a trusted financial advisor can be one of the best investments you make in protecting your legacy.

A good financial advisor starts by understanding your goals, values, and financial situation. They take the time to listen to your aspirations and concerns, creating a personalized plan that aligns with your objectives. Whether you're focused on growing your wealth, planning for retirement, or setting up an estate plan, a financial advisor can provide tailored advice and strategies to help you achieve your goals. This personalized approach ensures that your financial plan is as unique as you are.

Financial advisors offer a wide range of services, from investment management to estate planning. They can help you build and diversify your investment portfolio, ensuring that it aligns with your risk tolerance and long-term goals. Advisors also provide guidance on tax planning, helping you minimize your tax liability and maximize your savings. Their expertise in estate planning ensures that your wealth is distributed according to your wishes, with minimal taxes and legal complications.

One of the key benefits of working with a financial advisor is their ability to provide objective advice. They can help you stay focused on your long-term goals and avoid emotional decision-making. For example, during market downturns, an advisor can provide reassurance and perspective, helping you avoid the temptation to sell investments at a loss. This objective guidance is invaluable in maintaining a disciplined and strategic approach to wealth management.

Regular reviews and updates are a crucial part of working with a financial advisor. Your financial situation and goals will evolve over time, and your advisor can help you adjust your plan accordingly. Regular check-ins ensure that your strategy remains aligned with your objectives and that any changes in the financial landscape are taken into account. This proactive approach helps you stay on track and adapt to new opportunities and challenges.

Selecting the right financial advisor is essential. Look for advisors who are certified and have a fiduciary duty to act in your best interest. Check their credentials, experience, and client reviews. It's also important to find an advisor who you feel comfortable with and can trust. Building a strong, collaborative relationship with your advisor will enhance the effectiveness of your financial plan and give you peace of mind.

In conclusion, a financial advisor is a valuable partner in protecting and growing your legacy. They provide expertise, personalized advice, and objective guidance, helping you navigate the complexities of wealth management and legacy planning. By working with a trusted advisor, you can ensure that your financial plan is robust, adaptable, and aligned with your long-term goals. Investing in professional advice is a proactive step towards securing your financial future and preserving your legacy for generations to come.

## Monitoring and Adjusting Plans

Building and protecting a legacy is not a set-it-and-forget-it task. It requires ongoing attention, regular reviews, and adjustments to stay on course. Think of your legacy plan as a dynamic, living document that evolves with your life circumstances and the financial landscape. Regularly monitoring and adjusting your plans ensures that they remain relevant, effective, and aligned with your goals. Let's dive into how you can keep your legacy plan on track.

The first step in monitoring your legacy plan is setting a schedule for regular reviews. Annual reviews are a good starting point, but you should also revisit your plan after any major life events, such as marriage, divorce, the birth of a child, or significant financial changes. These reviews help you stay on top of your financial situation and make necessary adjustments to your strategy. Consider setting reminders in your calendar to ensure that these reviews happen consistently.

During your reviews, assess your financial goals and progress. Are you on track to meet your short-term and long-term objectives? If not, identify the areas that need adjustment. This might involve reallocating investments, increasing savings, or adjusting your budget. Keep in mind that your goals may evolve over time, so be flexible and willing to update them as needed. Regularly reviewing your progress keeps you accountable and motivated to achieve your financial aspirations.

Stay informed about changes in the financial landscape. Tax laws, investment opportunities, and economic conditions can all impact your legacy plan. Work with your financial advisor to stay updated on relevant changes and how they might affect your strategy. For example, changes in tax legislation could prompt you to adjust your estate plan or explore new tax-efficient investment options. Staying informed ensures that your plan remains effective and takes advantage of new opportunities.

Evaluate the performance of your investments. Are they meeting your expectations and aligned with your risk tolerance and goals? If certain investments are underperforming, it might be time to reallocate your assets. Diversification is key to managing risk, so ensure your portfolio remains well-balanced. Your financial advisor can help you analyze performance data and make informed decisions about buying, selling, or holding investments. Regularly tweaking your investment strategy helps optimize returns and protect your wealth.

Review your insurance coverage periodically. As your life changes, so do your insurance needs. Ensure that your life, health, disability, and property insurance policies provide adequate coverage for your current situation. For instance, if you've acquired new assets or expanded your family, you might need additional coverage. Regularly updating your insurance policies ensures that your legacy is protected against unforeseen events.

Update legal documents as needed. Wills, trusts, and other estate planning documents should reflect your current wishes and circumstances. Major life events or changes in family dynamics might necessitate updates to your beneficiaries, executors, or trustees. Ensuring that these documents are accurate and up-to-date prevents legal complications and ensures that your legacy is distributed according to your intentions.

Finally, communicate with your family about any changes to your legacy plan. Open communication fosters trust and understanding, ensuring that your family is aware of your wishes and prepared to manage your legacy. Discuss any updates or adjustments you've made and explain the reasons behind them. This transparency helps prevent misunderstandings and ensures a smooth transition when the time comes to pass on your legacy.

In summary, monitoring and adjusting your legacy plan is a continuous process that ensures its effectiveness and alignment with your evolving goals and circumstances. Regular reviews, staying informed, evaluating investments, updating insurance coverage, and keeping legal documents current are all crucial steps in maintaining a robust legacy plan. By staying proactive and adaptable, you can protect your wealth and ensure that your legacy endures for generations to come.

# Chapter 5
# The Inheritance for My Children's Children

## Planning for Future Generations

Planning for future generations is about more than just leaving money behind. It's about creating a lasting impact and ensuring that your descendants have the tools, knowledge, and resources to thrive. When I first thought about what I wanted to leave for my children's children, it became clear that a holistic approach was necessary—one that encompasses financial security, education, values, and family unity.

Start by defining what legacy means to you. Is it purely financial, or does it also include values, traditions, and education? For me, it was crucial to blend all these elements. I wanted my grandchildren to inherit not only wealth but also the principles and wisdom that guided our family. This holistic view ensures that your legacy provides a solid foundation for their future.

Financial planning is a key component of preparing for future generations. Establish trusts that can provide for your grandchildren's needs while protecting the assets from potential risks. Trusts can be structured to support education, healthcare, and even first-time home purchases. They can also include stipulations that encourage responsible financial behavior, such as matching contributions to savings or requiring the completion of certain educational milestones.

Education is a powerful legacy. Set up education funds for your grandchildren to ensure they have access to quality education without the burden of student debt. Whether it's a 529 plan or a trust specifically for education, making this investment shows your commitment to their future success. Encourage a love of learning by supporting extracurricular activities, educational travel, and enrichment programs. Education is a gift that keeps on giving, providing opportunities and opening doors throughout their lives.

Instilling values and traditions is equally important. Share your family history, stories, and traditions with your grandchildren. Create opportunities for family gatherings where these stories and values can be passed down. Encourage activities that build character, such as volunteering, participating in community events, and supporting causes that are important to your family. This nurtures a sense of identity and continuity, helping your grandchildren understand their roots and the values that define your family.

Consider the role of mentorship and guidance. Be actively involved in your grandchildren's lives, offering support and advice as they navigate their personal and professional journeys. Your experience and wisdom can provide valuable insights and help them avoid common pitfalls. Encourage open communication and be a trusted confidant. This involvement reinforces the bonds of family and ensures that your influence extends beyond material inheritance.

Finally, plan for the unexpected. Life is unpredictable, and having contingency plans in place ensures that your grandchildren are protected. This includes having adequate insurance, an updated estate plan, and clearly defined guardianship arrangements if needed. By anticipating potential challenges and preparing for them, you create a safety net that secures your grandchildren's future, regardless of what life throws their way.

## Teaching Financial Responsibility

Teaching financial responsibility to your grandchildren is one of the most valuable legacies you can provide. It's about equipping them with the skills and knowledge they need to make sound financial decisions throughout their lives. When I started this journey, I realized that financial literacy was just as crucial as leaving behind financial assets. By instilling good financial habits early, you set the stage for a lifetime of financial health and independence.

Start with the basics. Introduce your grandchildren to fundamental financial concepts such as saving, budgeting, and understanding the value of money. Use age-appropriate methods to make these lessons engaging and relatable. For younger children, a simple piggy bank can teach the importance of saving. As they grow older, involve them in family budgeting discussions and show them how to track expenses. These foundational skills are essential for developing a healthy relationship with money.

Encourage earning and saving. Teach your grandchildren the value of earning their own money through chores, part-time jobs, or entrepreneurial activities like lemonade stands or babysitting. This not only provides practical experience but also instills a sense of pride and accomplishment. Emphasize the importance of saving a portion of their earnings for future needs or goals. Consider matching their savings contributions to reinforce this habit and show your support for their financial growth.

Introduce the concept of investing. Explain how money can grow over time through smart investments. Start with simple examples, such as opening a savings account or purchasing a small amount of stock in a company they are interested in. As they get older, teach them about more complex investment vehicles like mutual funds, real estate, and retirement accounts. Encourage them to research and make informed decisions. Understanding investments early on sets the stage for building wealth and achieving financial independence.

Promote responsible spending. Teach your grandchildren how to distinguish between needs and wants and the importance of living within their means. Encourage them to make thoughtful spending decisions and avoid impulsive purchases. Discuss the benefits of budgeting and how it can help them achieve their financial goals. Provide real-life examples and involve them in planning family expenses. Responsible spending habits lead to financial stability and peace of mind.

Discuss the dangers of debt. Explain how debt can quickly become overwhelming and the importance of using credit wisely. Teach them about interest rates, minimum payments, and the long-term impact of carrying high-interest debt. Encourage them to pay off credit card balances in full each month and to avoid taking on unnecessary loans. Understanding the implications of debt helps them make smarter financial choices and avoid common pitfalls.

Lastly, lead by example. Your behavior and attitudes towards money will significantly influence your grandchildren. Demonstrate good financial habits in your own life, such as saving regularly, investing wisely, and living within your means. Share your experiences, both successes and mistakes, and the lessons you've learned. By being a positive financial role model, you provide a powerful example for your grandchildren to follow.

## Inheritance Laws

Understanding inheritance laws is crucial for ensuring that your legacy is passed down smoothly and according to your wishes. These laws vary significantly depending on your jurisdiction and can impact how your assets are distributed, taxed, and managed. When I began planning my estate, I realized the importance of navigating these laws to protect my family's future. Let's explore the key aspects of inheritance laws and how they can affect your legacy planning.

First, familiarize yourself with the basic concepts of inheritance law in your country or state. This includes understanding the difference between wills and trusts, how probate works, and the legal requirements for creating and executing these documents. Each jurisdiction has its own set of rules, and staying informed ensures that your estate plan is legally sound. Consulting with an estate planning attorney can provide clarity and ensure that you comply with all relevant laws.

A will is a fundamental document in inheritance law. It outlines how your assets should be distributed after your death and names an executor to carry out your wishes. Without a valid will, your estate will be subject to intestate succession laws, which dictate how your assets are divided among your heirs. These laws may not align with your preferences, so having a will is essential for ensuring that your wishes are honored. Regularly update your will to reflect changes in your family or financial situation.

Trusts offer additional benefits and flexibility in estate planning. They can help you manage and protect your assets during your lifetime and provide for your beneficiaries after your death. Trusts can also minimize estate taxes and avoid the probate process, which can be time-consuming and costly. Different types of trusts serve different purposes, such as revocable trusts, irrevocable trusts, and special needs trusts. Understanding the advantages and limitations of each type can help you choose the right trust for your needs.

Estate taxes can significantly impact the value of your inheritance. Depending on your jurisdiction, your estate may be subject to federal and state estate taxes. These taxes are calculated based on the total value of your estate and can reduce the amount your heirs receive. Implementing tax planning strategies, such as gifting assets during your lifetime, creating trusts, or purchasing life insurance, can help minimize estate taxes and preserve more of your wealth for your beneficiaries.

Probate is the legal process of validating a will and distributing an estate according to the will's terms. It involves court supervision and can be lengthy and expensive. Assets held in joint tenancy, payable-on-death accounts, and trusts typically bypass probate, allowing for quicker and more private distribution. Understanding which assets are subject to probate and structuring your estate to minimize its impact can simplify the inheritance process for your heirs.

Lastly, consider the impact of inheritance laws on your beneficiaries. Different types of inheritances can have various legal and tax implications for your heirs. For example, inheriting retirement accounts, real estate, or business interests can come with specific rules and tax considerations. Educate your beneficiaries about these implications and provide guidance on managing their inheritance responsibly. Clear communication and proper planning ensure that your legacy benefits your heirs without causing unnecessary legal or financial complications.

In summary, inheritance laws play a critical role in how your legacy is preserved and passed down. By understanding these laws and incorporating them into your estate planning, you can ensure that your assets are distributed according to your wishes, minimize taxes, and protect your family's future. Working with legal and financial professionals can provide the expertise and support needed to navigate the complexities of inheritance laws and create a comprehensive, effective estate plan.

## Teaching Financial Literacy Early

When it comes to building a legacy, teaching financial literacy early is one of the best gifts you can give your grandchildren. It's not just about leaving them money; it's about equipping them with the knowledge and skills they need to manage that money wisely. Financial literacy is the foundation of financial independence, and starting young makes all the difference.

Begin with simple concepts. Even young children can learn the basics of money—what it is, how it's used, and why it's important. Use everyday experiences as teaching moments. For instance, when you go shopping, explain how you decide what to buy and how much to spend. Show them how you save money for bigger purchases and how you avoid impulse buys. These small lessons add up over time and build a strong foundation.

As they get older, introduce more complex topics like budgeting and saving. Help them create their own budget using their allowance or money earned from chores. Teach them to set aside a portion for savings, a portion for spending, and a portion for giving. This not only teaches financial discipline but also the importance of generosity. Making these habits second nature early on will serve them well throughout their lives.

Open a savings account for them. Take them to the bank and explain how savings accounts work. Show them how their money can grow over time with interest. This hands-on experience can be incredibly powerful. They'll see the benefits of saving first-hand and understand the value of patience and planning. As they watch their savings grow, they'll be motivated to keep saving and making smart financial decisions.

Talk to them about the dangers of debt. Explain how credit cards work and the importance of paying off balances in full each month. Share stories of people who have struggled with debt and how it impacted their lives. Emphasize that while borrowing can be helpful, it's crucial to do so responsibly. Understanding debt early on helps them avoid common financial pitfalls and maintain a healthy financial life.

Introduce the concept of investing. Start with simple explanations of how stocks, bonds, and mutual funds work. Use examples of well-known companies to make it relatable. You might even help them buy a small amount of stock in a company they're interested in. This makes investing tangible and exciting. As they get older, delve deeper into investment strategies and the importance of diversification. Investing knowledge empowers them to grow their wealth effectively.

Finally, make financial literacy fun. Use games and apps designed to teach financial concepts. There are many resources available that make learning about money engaging and interactive. By keeping the learning process enjoyable, you're more likely to capture their interest and make the lessons stick. Remember, the goal is to instill a lifelong appreciation for smart money management, setting them up for a successful financial future.

## Creating a Family Financial Plan

Creating a family financial plan is a fantastic way to ensure everyone is on the same page about money matters. It's about setting goals, making decisions together, and building a united front when it comes to finances. When I started involving my family in financial planning, it not only brought us closer but also taught us all valuable lessons about money management.

Start by setting clear financial goals as a family. Sit down and discuss what you want to achieve in the short term and long term. These goals could range from saving for a family vacation to planning for college or retirement. Involving everyone in this process ensures that each family member feels valued and heard. Plus, it teaches your children the importance of goal setting and planning.

Break down your goals into actionable steps. For example, if your goal is to save for a family vacation, determine how much you need to save each month to reach your target. Assign responsibilities and track your progress regularly. This keeps everyone accountable and motivated. It's also a great way to teach children about budgeting and the importance of sticking to a plan.

Create a family budget. This involves listing all sources of income and all expenses, then finding ways to allocate your resources efficiently. Encourage everyone to participate in this process, even the kids. Show them how to track spending, identify areas where you can cut back, and prioritize savings. A family budget not only helps you manage your money better but also fosters teamwork and communication.

Incorporate saving and investing into your family plan. Decide on a percentage of your income to put towards savings and investments each month. This could include emergency funds, college savings accounts, or retirement funds. Explain to your children why saving and investing are important and how they can grow over time. Seeing these principles in action helps them understand the value of long-term financial planning.

Discuss the importance of giving and charitable contributions. Decide as a family how you want to give back to the community. This could be through monetary donations, volunteering, or supporting causes you care about. Teaching your children the importance of generosity and social responsibility is a vital part of financial literacy. It helps them understand that money is not just for personal gain but can be used to make a positive impact.

Review and adjust your family financial plan regularly. Life changes, and so should your plan. Make it a habit to review your goals, budget, and progress periodically. Celebrate your achievements and address any challenges together. This keeps your plan dynamic and adaptable, ensuring it continues to meet your family's needs. Regular reviews also provide opportunities for continuous learning and improvement in money management skills.

## Monitoring and Updating the Plan

Once you have a family financial plan in place, it's essential to monitor and update it regularly. A plan is only as good as its execution, and life's unpredictability means you'll need to make adjustments along the way. Think of your financial plan as a living document that evolves with your family's circumstances and goals.

Start by setting regular check-ins to review your financial plan. Monthly or quarterly reviews work well for most families. During these meetings, go over your budget, track your progress towards your goals, and discuss any changes in income or expenses. These check-ins help you stay on top of your finances and make necessary adjustments promptly.

They also keep everyone in the family engaged and informed.

Celebrate your progress and achievements. When you reach a financial milestone, whether it's paying off a debt, reaching a savings goal, or successfully sticking to your budget for a month, take the time to celebrate. Recognizing your successes keeps everyone motivated and reinforces the positive habits you've developed. It's a great way to show your children that hard work and discipline pay off.

Adjust your plan as needed. Life is full of unexpected events—job changes, medical expenses, new family members, or even shifts in your financial goals. Be flexible and willing to adapt your plan to accommodate these changes. For example, if you receive a bonus at work, decide as a family how to allocate that extra income. Should it go towards your emergency fund, a family vacation, or investing? Making these decisions together ensures everyone's priorities are considered.

Stay informed about financial trends and opportunities. The financial landscape is always changing, and staying educated helps you make better decisions. Read books, attend workshops, or follow financial news to keep up with new strategies and tools. Share this information with your family during your regular check-ins. Continuous learning not only improves your financial plan but also keeps everyone engaged and knowledgeable.

Revisit your goals periodically. As your family grows and evolves, so will your financial goals. What was important a few years ago might not be relevant now. Regularly reassess your short-term and long-term goals and adjust them as necessary. This ensures that your financial plan remains aligned with your family's current needs and aspirations. It also keeps the process dynamic and reflective of your evolving life.

Encourage open communication. Financial discussions should be a safe space where everyone feels comfortable sharing their thoughts and concerns. Encourage your family members to speak up if they have questions or if something isn't working. Addressing issues promptly and constructively prevents small problems from becoming significant obstacles. It also fosters a sense of teamwork and mutual support.

By monitoring and updating your family financial plan regularly, you ensure that it remains effective and relevant. This proactive approach helps you navigate life's uncertainties and keep your family on track towards achieving your financial goals. Remember, the goal is not just to have a plan, but to live it, adapt it, and make it a tool that truly supports your family's journey towards financial security and prosperity.

# Chapter 6
# What Does This Family House Look Like?

## Defining Family Values and Vision

Creating a family legacy begins with defining your family's values and vision. Think of these as the blueprint for the house you're building. What principles will guide your family? What kind of legacy do you want to leave behind? When I started this journey, I realized that clarity on these points was crucial. It's about knowing what you stand for and where you're headed.

Start by gathering your family together for a discussion. This could be around the dinner table or during a family meeting. Encourage everyone to share their thoughts and ideas about what's important to them. Talk about values such as honesty, integrity, generosity, and perseverance. Each family member's input is valuable, and this discussion helps to ensure that the family values and vision reflect everyone's beliefs and aspirations.

Once you've gathered input, distill these values into a clear, concise statement. This family mission statement will serve as your guiding star. For example, your statement might be, "Our family values honesty, hard work, and kindness. We strive to support each other and contribute positively to our community." This mission statement provides a shared understanding and direction, helping to align your family's actions and decisions with your core values.

Integrate these values into your daily life. It's one thing to talk about values; it's another to live them. Look for

70

opportunities to demonstrate and reinforce your family's values in everyday activities. For instance, if generosity is one of your core values, involve your family in volunteer work or charitable giving. If you value education, create a supportive environment for learning at home. Living your values makes them real and tangible for everyone in the family.

Vision goes hand in hand with values. Your family vision is a picture of what you want your future to look like. It encompasses your goals, dreams, and the impact you want to make. Encourage your family to dream big. What kind of life do you want to lead? What do you want to achieve together? What kind of legacy do you want to leave for future generations? These questions help shape a compelling vision that inspires and motivates everyone.

Write down your family vision and revisit it regularly. Life changes, and your vision might evolve over time. Regularly reviewing and updating your vision ensures that it remains relevant and reflects your family's current aspirations. This practice keeps everyone focused and aligned, reinforcing a sense of unity and purpose.

Finally, celebrate your values and vision. Make them a part of your family's identity. Display your mission statement and vision somewhere visible in your home. Celebrate milestones and achievements that align with your values. These celebrations reinforce the importance of your family's principles and keep everyone motivated to live up to them.

# Creating Family Traditions

Family traditions are the heartbeats that give rhythm to our lives and connect generations. They're like the bricks and mortar of your family house, providing structure, stability, and a sense of belonging. Traditions foster a sense of identity and continuity, helping to strengthen family bonds and create lasting memories. When I realized the power of traditions, I knew they had to be a cornerstone of our family legacy.

Start by identifying the traditions you already have. These could be holiday celebrations, birthday rituals, or simple routines like Sunday dinners. Discuss with your family which traditions are most meaningful and why. Understanding the significance of existing traditions helps you appreciate their value and ensures they continue to be cherished.

Next, think about new traditions you can create together. These can be big or small, elaborate or simple. The key is consistency and meaning. For example, you might start a tradition of family game night once a week, a yearly vacation to the same location, or a special way of celebrating achievements. In our family, we started a tradition of writing letters to each other on New Year's Eve, reflecting on the past year and sharing our hopes for the next. This tradition has become a cherished part of our family culture.

Involve everyone in the creation of new traditions. Encourage each family member to contribute ideas and participate in the planning. This involvement ensures that the traditions are meaningful to everyone and fosters a sense of ownership and pride. Traditions should evolve naturally, reflecting your family's unique personality and values. They should feel joyful and voluntary, not forced or obligatory.

Document your traditions. Take photos, keep a journal, or create a scrapbook to capture the memories. This documentation not only preserves your family's history but also allows you to relive those moments and pass them down to future generations. Looking back on these records can bring immense joy and reinforce the continuity of your traditions.

Adapt and evolve your traditions as needed. Life changes, and sometimes traditions need to be adjusted to fit new circumstances. Be flexible and open to modifications that keep traditions relevant and enjoyable. For instance, if your family grows or relocates, find new ways to celebrate old traditions or create new ones that suit your current situation. The essence of tradition lies in the shared experience, not necessarily the specific activity.

Finally, celebrate the role of traditions in your family. Recognize and honor the effort that goes into maintaining them. Share stories about past celebrations and the origins of your traditions with younger family members. This storytelling helps to pass down the meaning and significance of your traditions, ensuring they continue to be cherished for generations.

## Maintaining Strong Family Bonds

Maintaining strong family bonds is like ensuring the walls of your family house remain sturdy and supportive. Strong relationships are the foundation of a happy, resilient family. When I focused on strengthening our family bonds, I saw how it brought us closer and created a supportive environment where everyone felt valued and loved.

Open communication is the cornerstone of strong family bonds. Encourage regular, honest conversations where everyone feels heard and respected. Create a safe space where family members can express their thoughts and feelings without fear of judgment. This might be through regular family meetings, casual dinner table discussions, or one-on-one talks. Open communication fosters understanding, trust, and a sense of belonging.

Quality time is another essential ingredient. In our busy lives, it's easy to overlook the importance of spending time together. Make a conscious effort to carve out time for family activities. This could be as simple as watching a movie together, going for a walk, or cooking a meal as a team. The key is to be present and engaged, showing that you value and prioritize each other's company. These shared experiences build a reservoir of happy memories and strengthen your emotional connection.

Support each other's dreams and goals. Show genuine interest in what your family members are passionate about and find ways to encourage and support them. Whether it's attending a sports event, helping with a school project, or simply listening when they need to talk, your support demonstrates love and commitment. Celebrating each other's achievements and milestones reinforces the sense of a united, supportive family.

Resolve conflicts constructively. Disagreements are natural in any family, but how you handle them makes all the difference. Approach conflicts with empathy and a willingness to understand the other person's perspective. Focus on finding solutions rather than assigning blame. Encourage calm, respectful discussions and be willing to compromise. Resolving conflicts in a healthy way strengthens relationships and teaches valuable conflict-resolution skills.

Celebrate each other's uniqueness. Every family member brings something special to the table. Recognize and appreciate these individual strengths and differences. Encourage each person to express themselves and pursue their interests. This celebration of individuality within the context of a supportive family unit fosters self-esteem and a sense of belonging.

Lastly, practice gratitude and positivity. Make it a habit to express appreciation for each other. Highlight the positive aspects of your family life and focus on what you love about each other. This positive reinforcement builds a strong, resilient family culture. Start traditions like a gratitude jar where everyone can write down what they're thankful for and read them together regularly. Gratitude creates a positive atmosphere that nurtures strong family bonds.

By maintaining strong family bonds, you ensure that your family house is built on a foundation of love, trust, and mutual support. These bonds not only make life more enjoyable but also provide strength and resilience during challenging times. Through open communication, quality time, support, constructive conflict resolution, celebrating uniqueness, and practicing gratitude, you can create a close-knit family that stands the test of time.

# Home Environment and Atmosphere

Creating a warm, welcoming home environment is like adding cozy furnishings and decorations to your family house. The atmosphere in your home significantly impacts your family's well-being and relationships. When I focused on making our home a positive space, I noticed a profound difference in our daily interactions and overall happiness. Let's explore how to create a nurturing home environment that supports and uplifts everyone.

Start with physical space. Your home doesn't need to be perfect or luxurious, but it should be clean, organized, and comfortable. Clutter can create stress and chaos, so make a habit of regularly decluttering and organizing your living spaces. Involve the whole family in maintaining a tidy home. Create designated areas for different activities, such as a cozy reading nook, a family game area, or a peaceful spot for reflection and meditation. These spaces make your home functional and inviting.

Personalize your home with meaningful decor. Display family photos, artwork, and mementos that reflect your values and memories. These personal touches make your home feel uniquely yours and remind everyone of the love and connections that bind you. For example, we have a wall of framed photos from family vacations and special occasions. Every time we walk by, it brings back happy memories and reinforces our family bond.

Create a positive atmosphere through sensory elements. Light, color, and sound all play a role in shaping the mood of your home. Use natural light as much as possible, and consider warm, calming colors for your decor. Play soothing or uplifting music that everyone enjoys. Add plants or flowers to bring a touch of nature indoors. These small changes can significantly enhance the ambiance and make your home a place of comfort and joy.

Establish routines and rituals that promote a sense of stability and security. Daily routines, such as shared meals or bedtime stories, provide structure and predictability, which are especially important for children. Weekend rituals, like movie nights or family outings, create opportunities for bonding and relaxation. These routines and rituals create a sense of continuity and belonging, making your home a safe haven.

Encourage open communication and positivity within your home. Foster an environment where everyone feels comfortable expressing their thoughts and feelings. Practice active listening and show empathy and understanding. Use positive language and affirmations to build each other up. For instance, start each day with a positive affirmation or end it by sharing something you're grateful for. This practice cultivates a supportive and loving atmosphere.

Incorporate elements of fun and creativity. Make your home a place where laughter and joy are abundant. Encourage creative activities like drawing, crafting, or playing music together. Plan fun family games or spontaneous dance parties. These activities not only bring joy but also strengthen your family bond and create lasting memories. Remember, a happy home is a healthy home.

# The Role of Faith and Spirituality

Faith and spirituality can be the foundation stones of your family house, providing strength, guidance, and a sense of purpose. Integrating spiritual practices into your daily life can bring your family closer together and offer comfort and direction in times of need. For us, incorporating faith into our home life has been transformative, deepening our connections and grounding us in shared beliefs.

Start by making spiritual practices a regular part of your routine. This could include daily prayers, meditation, or reading and discussing spiritual texts. Find a time that works for everyone, whether it's in the morning, before meals, or at bedtime. These practices create moments of reflection and gratitude, fostering a sense of peace and unity. For example, we start each day with a short family prayer, setting a positive tone for the day ahead.

Attend religious services or spiritual gatherings together. Whether it's going to church, temple, mosque, or another place of worship, participating in communal activities reinforces your faith and provides a sense of belonging. It's also an opportunity to connect with a larger community that shares your values. Discuss the experiences and teachings from these gatherings with your family to deepen your understanding and application of your faith in everyday life.

Celebrate religious and spiritual holidays and milestones as a family. These occasions offer valuable opportunities to reinforce your faith and create lasting memories. Plan activities, meals, and rituals that involve everyone. For example, during holidays like Christmas or Hanukkah, involve your family in decorating, cooking, and giving back to the community. These shared experiences strengthen your bond and deepen your collective spiritual practice.

Encourage open discussions about faith and spirituality. Create a safe space where family members can share their beliefs, doubts, and experiences. Respect each other's perspectives and support one another's spiritual journeys. These discussions can be incredibly enriching and help each family member feel understood and valued. For instance, we have a tradition of discussing a different spiritual topic each week during dinner, which sparks meaningful conversations and mutual growth.

Model spiritual principles in your daily life. Demonstrate how faith guides your actions and decisions. Show kindness, patience, and forgiveness in your interactions. Your behavior sets a powerful example for your children and teaches them how to live out their faith. Share stories of how your spirituality has influenced your life, both the challenges and the triumphs. This transparency helps your family see the practical impact of faith and inspires them to integrate it into their own lives.

Lastly, engage in service and acts of kindness as a family. Volunteering and helping others are core aspects of many spiritual traditions. Find opportunities to serve your community, whether it's through organized volunteer work or simple acts of kindness. These activities reinforce the values of compassion and generosity and show your family the importance of living out their faith. It's a powerful way to connect with each other and the world around you.

## Balancing Individuality and Unity

Balancing individuality and unity within a family is like crafting the perfect blend of colors in a painting. Each member brings their unique hue, and together, they create a beautiful masterpiece. Encouraging individual expression while fostering a sense of unity can strengthen your family bond and create a harmonious home environment. When I focused on this balance, I saw our family flourish with each person feeling valued and connected.

Start by recognizing and celebrating each person's individuality. Encourage your family members to pursue their interests, hobbies, and passions. This might mean supporting one child's love for sports while nurturing another's artistic talents. Acknowledge and appreciate each person's unique contributions to the family. This recognition fosters self-esteem and a sense of belonging. For example, we have a tradition of celebrating "talent days" where each family member gets to showcase something they love doing, from playing an instrument to baking a cake.

Create opportunities for individual growth and development. Encourage your family members to set personal goals and support them in achieving those goals. This could involve taking classes, joining clubs, or simply dedicating time to practice their skills. Providing resources and encouragement for personal growth helps each person feel empowered and fulfilled. It also shows that you value their individuality and are invested in their success.

Foster a sense of unity through shared experiences and traditions. While celebrating individuality, it's equally important to create moments that bring everyone together. Plan regular family activities that everyone enjoys, such as game nights, movie marathons, or outdoor adventures. These shared experiences build a sense of togetherness and create lasting memories. In our family, we make it a point to have weekly "family fun days" where we do something enjoyable together, reinforcing our bond.

Encourage open communication and mutual respect. Create an environment where everyone feels comfortable expressing their thoughts and feelings. Practice active listening and show empathy towards each other's perspectives. This open dialogue fosters understanding and strengthens relationships. It's important to respect each person's individuality while emphasizing the value of family unity. For example, during our family meetings, we ensure that everyone has a chance to speak and be heard, promoting a culture of respect and inclusion.

Model the balance of individuality and unity in your behavior. Show your family how to pursue personal interests while contributing to the family's well-being. Demonstrate the importance of self-care and personal growth alongside family responsibilities and support. Your actions serve as a powerful example, teaching your children how to navigate this balance in their own lives. Share your own experiences of balancing personal and family priorities, highlighting the benefits of both.

Lastly, celebrate the collective achievements of your family. Recognize and honor the milestones and successes that you achieve together. Whether it's a family project, a group volunteer effort, or simply maintaining a harmonious home, celebrate these accomplishments as a team. This reinforces the idea that while each person's individuality is important, the strength of the family lies in its unity. For instance, when we complete a family project, we always take time to celebrate our teamwork and the combined effort that made it possible.

By balancing individuality and unity, you create a family environment where each person feels valued for who they are while being part of a supportive, cohesive unit. This balance fosters personal growth, mutual respect, and a deep sense of connection, building a strong and harmonious family legacy.

# Chapter 7
# Holy Ghost Help Me Decorate!

## Spiritual Guidance in Daily Life

Inviting spiritual guidance into your daily life is like adding the finishing touches to your family house—it brings everything together with purpose and meaning. When I began seeking the Holy Spirit's guidance in our everyday activities, it transformed the way we lived and interacted as a family. Let's explore how you can weave spiritual guidance into the fabric of your daily life, making it a natural and enriching part of your routine.

Start your day with prayer or meditation. Taking a few moments each morning to connect with the Holy Spirit sets a positive tone for the day. It's a time to seek guidance, express gratitude, and ask for strength and wisdom. Whether it's a quiet moment of reflection or a family prayer session, this practice can center your thoughts and align your actions with your spiritual values. For example, we begin each day with a simple prayer, asking for guidance and blessings for whatever lies ahead.

Incorporate spiritual readings into your routine. Whether it's scripture, inspirational books, or daily devotionals, reading spiritually uplifting material can provide insight and encouragement. Make it a habit to read and reflect on a passage each day, either individually or as a family. Discussing these readings can lead to meaningful conversations and deepen your understanding of spiritual principles. In our family, we often read a short devotional together during breakfast, sparking discussions that carry us through the day.

Seek the Holy Spirit's guidance in decision-making. When faced with choices, big or small, take a moment to pray and ask for wisdom. This practice helps you approach decisions with a clear mind and a humble heart, seeking what is best for your family and in alignment with your values. Trust that the Holy Spirit will guide you towards the right path. For example, when making significant decisions like changing jobs or moving, we take time to pray and reflect, seeking spiritual direction before proceeding.

Practice gratitude and mindfulness. Regularly acknowledging the blessings in your life can cultivate a positive and grateful mindset. Encourage your family to share what they are thankful for, whether during meals, bedtime, or family gatherings. Being mindful of the present moment and the beauty in everyday experiences helps you stay connected to the divine and appreciate the guidance and support you receive. We have a tradition of sharing our "gratitude moments" during dinner, where each person mentions something they are grateful for that day.

Involve the Holy Spirit in your interactions with others. Approach relationships with love, kindness, and empathy, guided by your spiritual principles. When conflicts arise, seek peace and understanding through prayer and reflection. Let your actions reflect the teachings of your faith, fostering a loving and supportive environment in your home and beyond. This approach not only strengthens your family bonds but also sets a positive example for others.

Create a spiritual space in your home. Dedicate a quiet corner or room for prayer, meditation, and reflection. This space can be adorned with meaningful symbols, comfortable seating, and inspirational materials. Having a designated area for spiritual practice reinforces its importance and provides a peaceful retreat from daily stresses. Our family has a small altar with candles, a cross, and a few cherished spiritual books, creating a serene space for connection and contemplation.

By inviting the Holy Spirit into your daily life, you infuse your family's routines with purpose, peace, and guidance. These practices help you navigate life's challenges with a centered heart and a clear mind, fostering a deeper connection with the divine and with each other. Embracing spiritual guidance enriches your family's journey and strengthens your collective bond.

## Creating a Spiritually Enriching Home

Creating a spiritually enriching home is like filling your house with warmth and light. It's about making your living space a reflection of your faith and values, a place where the Holy Spirit feels welcome and where your family can grow spiritually. When I started focusing on creating such an environment, it transformed our home into a sanctuary of peace and inspiration. Let's explore how you can make your home a spiritually enriching space.

Begin with intentional decor. Use items that have spiritual significance to decorate your home. This could include religious symbols, artwork, scriptures, or inspirational quotes. These items serve as constant reminders of your faith and values, creating an atmosphere that nurtures your spirit. For instance, we have framed scriptures in various rooms, which not only beautify our home but also provide daily encouragement and reflection.

Set up a family altar or prayer corner. This dedicated space can be a focal point for your family's spiritual practices. Include items that hold spiritual meaning for your family, such as candles, religious texts, icons, or flowers. Encourage family members to use this space for prayer, meditation, and reflection. It becomes a sacred area where you can retreat for spiritual nourishment and connection. Our family altar includes a cross, a Bible, and candles, creating a peaceful spot for contemplation.

Incorporate spiritual rituals into your daily routine. Rituals provide structure and meaning, grounding your family in your faith. This could include morning and evening prayers, blessing meals, or lighting candles for special intentions. These practices create moments of spiritual connection throughout the day, reinforcing your family's faith and unity. For example, we have a nightly ritual of lighting a candle and saying a prayer of gratitude before dinner, bringing us together in a moment of reflection and thankfulness.

Encourage spiritual conversations. Make it a habit to discuss spiritual topics during family gatherings. Share your experiences, insights, and questions about faith. These conversations deepen your understanding and strengthen your family's spiritual bond. They also create an open and supportive environment where everyone feels comfortable exploring their spirituality. During our family dinners, we often discuss a spiritual theme or question, leading to enriching and thought-provoking conversations.

Use music and media to enhance your spiritual atmosphere. Play uplifting and inspirational music that resonates with your faith. Watch movies or documentaries that inspire and educate. These media can reinforce spiritual messages and provide a shared experience for your family. We enjoy playing hymns or spiritual songs during family time, creating a joyful and reflective atmosphere.

Foster an attitude of service and compassion. Encourage your family to engage in acts of kindness and service, both within the home and in the community. This could include volunteering, helping a neighbor, or simply supporting each other's needs. Acts of service reflect the teachings of your faith and instill a sense of purpose and fulfillment. Our family participates in community service projects together, which strengthens our bond and helps us live out our values.

By creating a spiritually enriching home, you provide a nurturing environment where faith can flourish. These practices not only enhance your family's spiritual growth but also transform your home into a haven of peace, love, and inspiration. Embracing spirituality in your daily life enriches your family's journey and strengthens your collective bond with the divine.

## Celebrating Spiritual Milestones

Celebrating spiritual milestones is like marking significant points on your family's journey of faith. These moments provide opportunities to reflect, rejoice, and reaffirm your commitment to your spiritual path. When we started celebrating spiritual milestones more intentionally, it deepened our family's faith and created cherished memories. Let's explore how you can celebrate these important occasions and make them meaningful for your family.

Identify key spiritual milestones. These can include sacraments, religious ceremonies, anniversaries, or personal spiritual achievements. Common milestones might be baptisms, confirmations, first communions, weddings, or anniversaries of significant spiritual events. Recognizing these moments helps you honor their significance and reinforces your family's spiritual journey. In our family, we celebrate baptism anniversaries with a special prayer and a small gathering.

Plan meaningful celebrations. Tailor each celebration to reflect the importance of the milestone. This could involve a special family meal, a prayer service, or a gathering with friends and extended family. Incorporate rituals and traditions that hold spiritual significance. For example, lighting a candle, offering prayers, or reading a passage from a sacred text can add depth and meaning to the celebration. For confirmations, we often hold a blessing ceremony followed by a family meal to celebrate the occasion.

Involve everyone in the preparations. Engaging the whole family in planning and preparing for these milestones makes the celebrations more meaningful. Assign roles and tasks, such as decorating, cooking, or leading prayers. This involvement fosters a sense of ownership and participation, making the celebration a shared experience. When preparing for a significant anniversary, we collaborate on everything from creating invitations to planning the service, ensuring everyone feels included.

Create lasting memories. Document these milestones with photos, videos, or written reflections. These records become treasured keepsakes that you can revisit and share with future generations. Consider creating a family scrapbook or digital album to preserve these memories. We have a family scrapbook where we add photos and notes from each milestone, allowing us to look back and reflect on our spiritual journey.

Reflect on the significance of the milestone. Take time to discuss and reflect on what the milestone means to your family and each individual. Share stories, experiences, and feelings associated with the event. This reflection deepens your understanding and appreciation of the spiritual journey. After a milestone celebration, we often sit down and share our thoughts and feelings, reinforcing the importance of the occasion and what it represents.

Give thanks and express gratitude. Use these milestones as opportunities to thank the Holy Spirit for guidance and blessings. Expressing gratitude fosters a positive and thankful mindset, enhancing your family's spiritual connection. We make it a point to include a moment of gratitude in each celebration, thanking the Holy Spirit for the journey so far and asking for continued guidance.

By celebrating spiritual milestones, you create meaningful and memorable experiences that reinforce your family's faith and unity. These celebrations not only honor significant moments but also provide opportunities for reflection, gratitude, and growth. Embracing and celebrating these milestones enriches your family's spiritual journey and strengthens your collective bond with the divine.

## Integrating Faith into Family Activities

Integrating faith into family activities is like weaving threads of spirituality into the fabric of your daily life. It's about making faith a natural and enjoyable part of your family's routine. When I began incorporating spiritual elements into our everyday activities, it brought a new level of meaning and joy to our time together. Let's explore how you can seamlessly blend faith into your family's activities.

Start with your family meals. Meals are a natural time to come together and share not just food, but also faith. Begin each meal with a prayer of thanks, asking for blessings on the food and each other. This simple act sets a positive tone and reminds everyone of the spiritual connection. During the meal, encourage discussions about your day, your blessings, and any spiritual insights. For example, we often share a "gratitude moment" where each person mentions something they are thankful for that day.

Incorporate faith into your outdoor activities. Whether it's a hike, a picnic, or a day at the park, use these moments to connect with nature and the divine. Take time to appreciate the beauty around you and acknowledge it as part of God's creation. You can say a prayer of gratitude for the natural world or read a scripture that speaks to the beauty of creation. These activities not only bring your family closer to nature but also deepen your spiritual appreciation.

Turn your family game nights into opportunities for faith-based fun. Choose games that incorporate spiritual themes or values. For example, Bible trivia games or charades with biblical characters can be both entertaining and educational. These games provide a fun way to reinforce your faith and learn more about your spiritual heritage. We enjoy playing a Bible-themed version of Pictionary, which always leads to laughter and learning.

Make service projects a regular family activity. Volunteering together as a family not only helps those in need but also reinforces the values of compassion and generosity. Choose projects that resonate with your family's values, such as serving at a soup kitchen, participating in a charity walk, or helping out at your place of worship. Discuss the spiritual significance of your service and how it aligns with your faith. Our family volunteers at a local food bank once a month, and it has become a meaningful way to live out our faith in action.

Integrate faith into your family's creative activities. Encourage your children to express their spirituality through art, music, and writing. This could involve drawing or painting scenes from religious stories, writing poems or songs about faith, or creating crafts that symbolize spiritual themes. Display these creations in your home as a reminder of your family's faith journey. We have a dedicated "faith wall" where we hang our children's spiritual artwork, celebrating their creativity and spiritual expression.

Involve faith in your family's holiday traditions. Whether it's Christmas, Easter, Hanukkah, or other religious holidays, make these celebrations rich with spiritual meaning. Attend religious services together, create special rituals, and discuss the significance of these holidays. Incorporate faith-based stories, songs, and prayers into your celebrations. For example, during Christmas, we have a tradition of reading the Nativity story before opening gifts, focusing on the true meaning of the holiday.

By integrating faith into your family activities, you create a seamless blend of spirituality and daily life. These practices make faith a living, dynamic part of your routine, enriching your family's experiences and strengthening your spiritual bond. Embracing faith in everyday activities deepens your connection with each other and with the divine, fostering a harmonious and spiritually fulfilling family life.

## The Power of Prayer in Family Life

Prayer is the cornerstone of a spiritually connected family. It's like the glue that holds your family house together, providing strength, guidance, and unity. When we made prayer a central part of our family life, it transformed our relationships and brought a deeper sense of peace and purpose. Let's explore how you can harness the power of prayer to enrich your family life.

Start by establishing regular family prayer times. Whether it's in the morning, before meals, or at bedtime, having set times for prayer creates a consistent routine. These moments provide opportunities to connect with each other and with the divine. Begin with simple, heartfelt prayers, and encourage each family member to take turns leading. This practice fosters a sense of shared responsibility and participation. In our family, we start and end each day with a brief prayer, setting a positive tone for the day and reflecting on our blessings at night.

Encourage spontaneous prayers throughout the day. Prayer doesn't have to be confined to specific times; it can be a natural response to life's moments. Teach your family to pray in times of joy, gratitude, concern, or need. This habit of turning to prayer in various situations reinforces a constant connection with the Holy Spirit. For example, when faced with a challenge, we pause to pray for guidance and strength, reminding ourselves of the divine presence in our lives.

Create a family prayer journal. This journal can be a place to write down prayer requests, thanksgivings, and reflections. It serves as a tangible record of your spiritual journey together. Encourage everyone to contribute, and review the journal regularly to see how prayers have been answered. This practice not only strengthens your faith but also provides a beautiful keepsake of your family's spiritual growth. Our family prayer journal is filled with entries that remind us of the power and faithfulness of prayer.

Incorporate different forms of prayer. Explore various prayer practices to keep your family's prayer life dynamic and engaging. This could include traditional prayers, meditative silence, praying with scripture, or even creative expressions like prayer through music or art. Introducing variety prevents prayer from becoming monotonous and helps each family member find their unique way of connecting with the divine. Sometimes, we play instrumental music and sit in silent prayer, allowing each person to commune with God in their own way.

Pray for each other. Make it a habit to pray for the needs and concerns of your family members. This practice fosters empathy, support, and a deep sense of unity. During family prayer times, ask each person to share their prayer requests and take turns praying for one another. This reinforces the importance of mutual care and strengthens your family bond. Knowing that we are prayed for by our loved ones provides immense comfort and encouragement.

Extend your prayers to the wider community. Encourage your family to pray for friends, neighbors, and the world at large. This outward focus broadens your perspective and nurtures a sense of compassion and interconnectedness. Discuss current events and issues, and incorporate prayers for those affected. This practice not only enriches your prayer life but also instills a sense of responsibility and service. We often include prayers for our community and global concerns, teaching our children to care for the world beyond our home.

By harnessing the power of prayer in your family life, you create a foundation of faith, love, and unity. Prayer becomes a source of strength and guidance, enriching your relationships and providing a constant connection with the divine. Embracing prayer in its many forms fosters a spiritually vibrant and resilient family, capable of facing life's challenges with grace and confidence.

## Encouraging Spiritual Growth

Encouraging spiritual growth within your family is like nurturing a garden—it requires attention, patience, and care. When I focused on fostering spiritual development in our home, I saw each family member flourish in their unique faith journey. Let's explore how you can create an environment that supports and encourages spiritual growth for everyone in your family.

Begin by setting a personal example. Your own spiritual journey can inspire and guide your family. Share your experiences, insights, and the practices that nourish your faith. Let your family see your commitment to spiritual growth through your actions, whether it's regular prayer, reading spiritual texts, or participating in faith-based activities. Your enthusiasm and dedication can motivate others to explore and deepen their own spirituality. I often share my spiritual readings and reflections during family time, sparking interest and curiosity in my children.

Provide resources for spiritual exploration. Offer a variety of books, podcasts, and videos that cover different aspects of spirituality. Encourage your family to explore these resources and find what resonates with them. Create a family library or a digital collection of spiritual materials. This accessibility makes it easy for everyone to engage with their faith at their own pace. Our family library includes a mix of spiritual classics, modern writings, and children's books, catering to all ages and interests.

Foster an environment of continuous learning. Encourage questions and discussions about faith. Create opportunities for your family to learn and grow together, such as attending spiritual retreats, workshops, or seminars. These experiences can provide fresh perspectives and deepen your collective understanding of spiritual principles. We often attend family retreats and seminars, which offer valuable insights and shared spiritual experiences.

Celebrate spiritual milestones and achievements. Acknowledge and honor the spiritual growth and achievements of each family member. This could include completing a spiritual course, participating in a religious ceremony, or reaching a personal spiritual goal. Celebrating these milestones reinforces the importance of spiritual growth and provides encouragement to continue the journey. For instance, we recently celebrated our daughter's completion of a Bible study course with a special family dinner and a certificate of achievement.

Create opportunities for service and giving. Engage your family in acts of kindness and service to others. Volunteering and charitable activities are powerful ways to live out your faith and develop a deeper sense of purpose. Discuss the spiritual significance of these actions and reflect on the experiences together. Our family regularly volunteers at a local shelter, and these activities have become a meaningful part of our spiritual practice.

Encourage personal spiritual practices. Support each family member in finding and cultivating their own spiritual practices. This could include prayer, meditation, journaling, or creative expressions like art or music. Provide the time and space for these practices to flourish. Respect and appreciate each person's unique journey, understanding that spiritual growth is deeply personal and varied.

# Chapter 8
# Navigating Life's Challenges with Faith

## Finding Strength in Adversity

Life is full of ups and downs, and it's during the challenging times that our faith can be a source of immense strength. When faced with adversity, turning to the Holy Spirit for guidance and support can help us navigate through the storm with resilience and grace. Reflecting on my own experiences, I've learned that faith can transform how we handle life's toughest moments. Let's explore how you can find strength in adversity through your faith.

Start by acknowledging your feelings. It's important to recognize and accept the emotions that come with difficult situations—whether it's fear, sadness, anger, or confusion. Bottling up these feelings can make the situation harder to bear. Instead, bring your emotions to God in prayer. Expressing your feelings openly can be incredibly liberating and helps you feel understood and supported. When our family faced a significant loss, we spent time in prayer, sharing our grief and seeking comfort.

Lean on scripture and spiritual texts. The Bible and other spiritual writings offer wisdom, encouragement, and hope during tough times. Find passages that speak to your situation and meditate on them. Reflect on stories of resilience and faith, and let them inspire you. For example, when I feel overwhelmed, I turn to Psalm 23, which reassures me of God's presence and guidance through life's valleys. Sharing these scriptures with your family can also provide collective strength and reassurance.

Pray for strength and guidance. Prayer is a powerful tool for finding strength in adversity. Ask the Holy Spirit for courage, wisdom, and resilience to face your challenges. Trust that you are not alone and that divine support is always available. Encourage your family to join you in prayer, creating a united front in seeking strength and comfort. In our family, we have a tradition of holding hands and praying together during difficult times, which brings us closer and strengthens our faith.

Seek support from your faith community. Surrounding yourself with others who share your beliefs can provide a strong support network. Reach out to your church, spiritual group, or trusted friends for prayer, advice, and encouragement. Sharing your burdens with others can lighten the load and provide different perspectives and insights. When we faced a health crisis, our church community offered prayers, meals, and emotional support, reminding us that we were not alone.

Focus on gratitude and positivity. Even in the darkest times, there are always things to be grateful for. Practicing gratitude can shift your focus from what's wrong to what's right, providing a sense of hope and perspective. Encourage your family to find something to be thankful for each day, no matter how small. This practice can uplift your spirits and strengthen your resolve. During a particularly tough period, we started a gratitude journal, noting down daily blessings, which helped us maintain a positive outlook.

Embrace resilience and adaptability. Life's challenges often require us to adapt and find new ways of coping. Lean on your faith to build resilience and the ability to bounce back from setbacks. Remember that adversity can be a powerful teacher, providing opportunities for growth and strengthening your character. Reflect on past challenges and how you overcame them with faith, using those experiences to bolster your confidence in facing current difficulties.

By finding strength in adversity through your faith, you can navigate life's challenges with courage and grace. These practices not only help you cope with immediate difficulties but also build a foundation of resilience and trust in the divine. Embracing faith in tough times enriches your journey and strengthens your spiritual bond with your family and the Holy Spirit.

## Embracing Change with Faith

Change is a constant in life, and how we respond to it can shape our experiences and growth. Embracing change with faith allows us to navigate transitions with hope and confidence. Reflecting on my own journey, I've seen how faith can turn uncertainty into opportunity and fear into trust. Let's explore how you can embrace change with faith and make it a positive force in your family's life.

Start by accepting that change is inevitable. Whether it's a new job, moving to a new city, or changes in family dynamics, understanding that change is a natural part of life can help you approach it with a more open mind. Accepting change doesn't mean you have to like it, but it does mean you recognize its role in your growth. In our family, we often remind each other that change, while challenging, can lead to new and exciting opportunities.

Turn to prayer for guidance and reassurance. When facing change, pray for clarity, strength, and the ability to see the positives in the new situation. Ask the Holy Spirit to help you navigate the transition with grace and trust. Prayer can provide a sense of peace and reassurance, reminding you that you are supported and guided. We make it a habit to pray together when anticipating big changes, asking for wisdom and courage to embrace what lies ahead.

Reflect on past experiences. Think about previous changes you've gone through and how you managed them. What did you learn? How did your faith help you? Reflecting on past experiences can provide valuable insights and build confidence in your ability to handle future changes. Share these reflections with your family to inspire and encourage them. For example, we often talk about our move to a new city and how it ultimately brought us closer and opened up new opportunities.

Maintain a positive attitude. Change can be daunting, but focusing on the potential positives can make the transition smoother. Look for the opportunities that change brings—new experiences, personal growth, and fresh perspectives. Encourage your family to adopt a positive mindset, emphasizing that change can lead to new blessings and adventures. When facing change, we try to highlight the exciting possibilities and focus on the potential for growth and improvement.

Stay flexible and adaptable. Change often requires us to adjust our routines and expectations. Embrace flexibility and be willing to adapt to new circumstances. Trust that the Holy Spirit is guiding you through these changes and that you have the strength to handle whatever comes your way. Encourage your family to be open to new experiences and to view change as an opportunity for growth. We often remind each other that being adaptable makes us stronger and more resilient.

Lean on your faith community. During times of change, your faith community can provide support, encouragement, and practical help. Share your experiences and concerns with trusted members of your community, and seek their prayers and advice. Being part of a supportive community can make transitions feel less isolating and more manageable. When we went through a major life change, our faith community provided invaluable support and encouragement, helping us navigate the transition with confidence.

By embracing change with faith, you can turn transitions into opportunities for growth and positive transformation. These practices help you and your family navigate changes with resilience and hope, strengthening your spiritual bond and trust in the divine. Embracing change with faith enriches your journey and empowers you to face the future with confidence and grace.

## Overcoming Fear and Anxiety

Fear and anxiety can be overwhelming, but turning to faith can provide the strength and peace needed to overcome these emotions. When I faced my own struggles with fear and anxiety, relying on my faith transformed my perspective and helped me find calm in the storm. Let's explore how you can use faith to overcome fear and anxiety and create a sense of peace for yourself and your family.

Start by acknowledging your fears and anxieties. It's important to recognize these feelings rather than suppressing them. Acknowledging your emotions is the first step towards addressing them. Share your fears with the Holy Spirit in prayer, asking for comfort and guidance. When we face anxious moments, we gather as a family to openly discuss our feelings and support each other through prayer and encouragement.

Turn to scripture for comfort and reassurance. The Bible is filled with passages that offer peace and hope in times of fear. Verses like Isaiah 41:10, "Do not fear, for I am with you; do not be dismayed, for I am your God," can provide immense comfort. Meditate on these scriptures and let their words calm your spirit. Reading these passages together as a family can also provide collective reassurance. We have a list of go-to verses that we read aloud when anxiety strikes, reminding us of God's constant presence and support.

Practice deep breathing and meditation. These techniques can help calm your mind and body, making it easier to focus on your faith and find peace. Take slow, deep breaths, and use each exhale to release tension and fear. Combine this practice with prayer or meditation on a comforting scripture. Encouraging your family to practice these techniques can create a more peaceful home environment. We often use guided meditation apps that incorporate scripture and prayer, finding it helps us relax and center ourselves.

Engage in physical activity. Exercise is a powerful tool for reducing anxiety and improving overall well-being. Encourage your family to stay active through activities they enjoy, such as walking, biking, or playing sports. Physical activity releases endorphins, which can help alleviate anxiety and promote a sense of calm. We make it a point to go for family walks or bike rides, using the time to connect with each other and nature, which helps us feel more grounded and relaxed.

Focus on gratitude. Shifting your focus from what you fear to what you're grateful for can help reduce anxiety. Encourage your family to keep a gratitude journal, noting down things they are thankful for each day. Reflecting on these blessings can provide perspective and remind you of the positives in your life. During anxious times, we gather as a family to share our gratitude lists, which helps us shift our focus from fear to thankfulness.

Create a support network. Surround yourself with people who uplift and encourage you. Share your fears and anxieties with trusted friends, family members, or members of your faith community. Their support and prayers can provide strength and reassurance. Knowing you are not alone in your struggles can make a significant difference. When anxiety hits, I reach out to a close friend for a comforting conversation and prayer, which always helps me feel more supported.

## Building Resilience Through Faith

Resilience is the ability to bounce back from adversity and keep moving forward, and faith plays a crucial role in developing this strength. When I started focusing on building resilience through faith, I noticed a significant change in how our family handled challenges. Let's explore how you can foster resilience within your family, using faith as your foundation.

Start by cultivating a positive mindset. Faith can help shift your perspective from fear and despair to hope and possibility. Encourage your family to focus on the positives, even in difficult situations. Remind them that challenges are opportunities for growth and that with God's help, they can overcome anything. In our family, we practice finding silver linings in tough times, reinforcing that every challenge has a purpose and can lead to greater strength.

Encourage a sense of purpose. Having a strong sense of purpose can provide direction and motivation during challenging times. Help your family identify their passions and strengths, and encourage them to use these gifts to serve others and contribute to the community. This sense of purpose can be a powerful source of resilience. We often volunteer together, finding that helping others reinforces our sense of purpose and strengthens our resolve.

Teach problem-solving skills. Resilience involves being able to face challenges head-on and finding solutions. Encourage your family to approach problems with a solution-focused mindset. Discuss potential strategies and support each other in brainstorming ideas. Faith can provide the confidence and clarity needed to tackle problems effectively. When faced with a difficult situation, we gather as a family to pray for guidance and then brainstorm practical solutions together.

Promote self-care and well-being. Physical and emotional health are essential for resilience. Encourage healthy habits such as regular exercise, balanced nutrition, adequate sleep, and time for relaxation and reflection. Taking care of your body and mind helps you stay strong and better equipped to handle stress. Our family has incorporated regular physical activity into our routine, finding that it boosts our mood and energy levels, making us more resilient.

Foster supportive relationships. Resilience is strengthened through strong, supportive relationships. Encourage open communication, empathy, and mutual support within your family. Create a network of friends and community members who can provide additional support. Knowing you have a reliable support system can make it easier to face and overcome challenges. We prioritize spending quality time together, ensuring that our family bonds remain strong and supportive.

Model resilience through your actions. Demonstrate resilience in your own life by handling challenges with grace and faith. Share your experiences and the lessons you've learned with your family. Your behavior sets a powerful example, showing them that it's possible to navigate tough times with strength and faith. I often share stories of my own struggles and how faith helped me overcome them, inspiring my family to develop their own resilience.

By building resilience through faith, you empower your family to face life's challenges with confidence and strength. These practices not only help you navigate immediate difficulties but also create a foundation of resilience that supports long-term growth and well-being. Embracing faith as a source of resilience enriches your family's journey and strengthens your collective ability to overcome adversity.

## Seeking Guidance from Spiritual Mentors

Spiritual mentors can provide invaluable support and wisdom, helping you navigate life's challenges with faith and insight. When I sought guidance from spiritual mentors, it opened new perspectives and strengthened my faith. Let's explore how you can benefit from the wisdom of spiritual mentors and integrate their guidance into your family's life.

Identify potential mentors. Look for individuals who embody the values and qualities you admire, and who have a deep understanding of your faith. These could be religious leaders, experienced members of your faith community, or even respected friends or family members. The key is finding someone who can offer guidance, support, and a different perspective. In our family, we identified a few trusted individuals whose faith and wisdom we greatly respect and sought their mentorship.

Build a relationship with your mentor. Approach your potential mentor with respect and openness, expressing your desire for guidance. Be honest about your challenges and the areas where you seek support. Building a trusting and open relationship is essential for effective mentorship. Regularly check in with your mentor, whether through meetings, phone calls, or emails. I found that scheduling monthly meetings with my mentor provided consistent support and deepened our relationship.

Be open to learning and growth. A good mentor will challenge you to think differently and push you out of your comfort zone. Be open to their feedback and willing to reflect on their insights. Apply their advice to your life and observe the changes. This openness to growth is crucial for personal and spiritual development. Whenever my mentor suggests new practices or perspectives, I make a conscious effort to incorporate them and reflect on their impact.

Involve your family in the mentorship process. Share the guidance you receive with your family and encourage them to seek their own mentors. Discuss the insights and lessons learned, and explore how they can be applied to your family's life. This collective learning fosters a shared journey of growth and faith. We often have family discussions about the advice and wisdom from our mentors, integrating their guidance into our daily lives.

Show appreciation and respect. Mentorship is a two-way relationship, and expressing gratitude is important. Acknowledge the time, effort, and wisdom your mentor provides. A simple thank-you note, a small gift, or a heartfelt conversation can go a long way in showing your appreciation. We make it a point to regularly thank our mentors and show our appreciation for their support and guidance.

Reflect on your mentorship journey. Take time to reflect on the impact of mentorship on your life and faith. Consider how your perspectives have changed, the growth you've experienced, and the challenges you've overcome with your mentor's help. This reflection can deepen your appreciation for the mentorship relationship and reinforce the lessons learned. I keep a journal where I document the insights and growth from my mentorship journey, which helps me track my progress and stay motivated.

By seeking guidance from spiritual mentors, you tap into a wealth of wisdom and experience that can enhance your faith journey. These relationships provide support, challenge you to grow, and offer new perspectives on life's challenges. Embracing mentorship enriches your family's spiritual journey and strengthens your collective faith and resilience.

## Cultivating Hope and Positivity

Cultivating hope and positivity is essential for navigating life's challenges with faith and grace. A hopeful and positive mindset can transform how you perceive and respond to difficulties. When I focused on fostering hope and positivity within our family, it brought a renewed sense of purpose and joy. Let's explore how you can cultivate these attitudes in your family life, enhancing your spiritual journey.

Begin each day with gratitude. Starting the day with a grateful heart sets a positive tone and shifts your focus from what's lacking to what's abundant. Encourage your family to share something they are thankful for each morning. This practice fosters a mindset of appreciation and optimism. In our family, we begin each day by sharing one thing we are grateful for, which helps us start the day on a positive note.

Surround yourself with positive influences. Fill your home with uplifting music, inspirational books, and encouraging messages. Choose media that reinforces hope and positivity. Limit exposure to negative news and content that can bring down your spirits. Creating a positive environment helps maintain an optimistic outlook. We have a playlist of uplifting songs that we play during breakfast, setting a joyful tone for the day.

Practice affirmations. Affirmations are positive statements that can help you challenge and overcome negative thoughts. Encourage your family to create and repeat affirmations that resonate with them. These statements can reinforce self-belief and a hopeful mindset. For example, we have a family affirmation board where each of us writes positive affirmations that we repeat daily, such as "I am strong, I am loved, and I can handle any challenge."

Focus on solutions, not problems. When faced with challenges, shift the focus from the problem to potential solutions. Encourage creative thinking and problem-solving within your family. This proactive approach fosters hope and confidence in your ability to overcome obstacles. During our family meetings, we discuss challenges and brainstorm solutions together, empowering each member to contribute ideas and take action.

Celebrate small victories. Recognize and celebrate progress, no matter how small. Acknowledging these moments reinforces a positive mindset and encourages continued effort. Celebrating small wins helps build momentum and keeps hope alive. We make it a point to celebrate achievements, whether it's completing a project, reaching a goal, or simply making it through a tough day with a positive attitude.

Cultivate a hopeful perspective through prayer and meditation. Use prayer and meditation to reinforce hope and trust in the divine. Ask for guidance and strength to maintain a positive outlook, even in challenging times. Reflect on scriptures and spiritual teachings that emphasize hope and resilience. Our family often meditates on verses like Jeremiah 29:11, "For I know the plans I have for you," declares the Lord, "plans to prosper you and not to harm you, plans to give you hope and a future."

Support each other in maintaining hope and positivity. Encourage open conversations about feelings and experiences, providing a supportive space for expressing concerns and finding encouragement. Lift each other up with kind words and gestures. Being each other's cheerleaders fosters a strong, supportive family environment. We make it a habit to check in with each other regularly, offering encouragement and support whenever needed.

By cultivating hope and positivity, you create a resilient and joyful family environment. These practices help you navigate life's challenges with a hopeful heart and a positive attitude, enriching your spiritual journey and strengthening your family bonds. Embracing hope and positivity enhances your family's ability to face adversity with faith and grace, making every day a step forward on your spiritual path.

## Engaging with Your Local Faith Community

Engaging with your local faith community is like adding a strong support beam to your family house. It provides additional strength, support, and a sense of belonging. When we became more involved in our local faith community, we experienced a deeper connection to our faith and found a network of support. Let's explore how you can engage with your local faith community and strengthen your family's spiritual journey.

Start by attending regular services. Being present at weekly worship services or gatherings is a simple yet powerful way to connect with your faith community. Regular attendance helps you stay grounded in your faith, provides spiritual nourishment, and fosters a sense of belonging. Encourage your family to participate actively in these services, whether it's through singing, prayer, or listening attentively to sermons. In our family, attending Sunday services together has become a cherished routine that reinforces our faith and unity.

Get involved in community activities. Many faith communities offer a variety of activities, such as Bible studies, prayer groups, volunteer opportunities, and social events. Participate in these activities to build relationships and deepen your involvement. These gatherings provide opportunities to learn, grow, and serve alongside others who share your beliefs. For example, we joined a weekly Bible study group that not only strengthened our understanding of scripture but also connected us with like-minded individuals.

Volunteer your time and talents. Serving your faith community is a wonderful way to give back and build meaningful connections. Look for opportunities to volunteer, whether it's helping with events, teaching classes, or supporting outreach programs. Volunteering allows you to use your skills and talents to benefit others and reinforces the values of compassion and service. Our family regularly volunteers at church events and community outreach programs, which has deepened our commitment to serving others.

Build relationships within your community. Take the time to get to know other members of your faith community. Engage in conversations, invite them over for meals, and participate in small group activities. Building personal connections fosters a sense of camaraderie and mutual support. These relationships can provide encouragement, advice, and friendship, enriching your spiritual journey. We often host potluck dinners, inviting members of our church to share a meal and fellowship, strengthening our bonds.

Support and pray for each other. One of the greatest strengths of a faith community is the support and prayer you can offer each other. Share your prayer requests and needs, and commit to praying for others. Knowing that you are supported in prayer provides comfort and strength. Similarly, offering your prayers and support to others builds a strong, caring community. In our church, we have a prayer chain where members can share their requests and commit to praying for each other, creating a powerful network of support.

Participate in faith community initiatives. Many faith communities have initiatives and programs aimed at addressing social issues, providing education, or supporting local needs. Get involved in these initiatives to make a positive impact and demonstrate your commitment to living out your faith. Whether it's participating in a food drive, supporting a mission trip, or advocating for social justice, your involvement makes a difference. We actively participate in our church's outreach programs, finding fulfillment in contributing to our community's well-being.

By engaging with your local faith community, you build a network of support, deepen your spiritual practice, and create meaningful connections. These activities not only strengthen your faith but also enrich your family's spiritual journey and foster a sense of belonging. Embracing your faith community enhances your ability to live out your values and make a positive impact on those around you.

## Building Relationships with Other Families

Building relationships with other families within your faith community is like expanding your family house to include a larger, supportive network. These connections provide additional support, friendship, and opportunities for mutual growth. When we started building relationships with other families, it enriched our spiritual journey and created a sense of extended family. Let's explore how you can build these relationships and create a strong, faith-filled network.

Start by reaching out. Take the initiative to introduce yourself to other families at your place of worship or faith-based events. Look for common interests and experiences to build a connection. A friendly conversation can be the starting point for a lasting relationship. In our family, we make it a point to introduce ourselves to new families at church, making them feel welcome and included.

Organize family-friendly activities. Plan events or gatherings that encourage families to come together and get to know each other. This could include potluck dinners, game nights, picnics, or outings. These activities provide a relaxed and enjoyable environment for building relationships. For example, we started a monthly family game night at our church, where families can come together for fun and fellowship.

Join or create small groups. Small groups or study groups offer a more intimate setting for building deeper connections. Join an existing group or start one focused on family, parenting, or specific interests. These groups provide a space for sharing experiences, discussing faith, and supporting each other. We joined a parenting small group, which has been invaluable for sharing advice, experiences, and spiritual support.

Participate in family-oriented faith programs. Many faith communities offer programs and classes specifically designed for families. These programs can provide valuable opportunities for learning, growth, and connection. Whether it's a family Bible study, a parenting class, or a family retreat, participating in these programs can strengthen your faith and relationships. We attended a family retreat organized by our church, which brought us closer to other families and deepened our faith.

Support each other's children. Building relationships with other families includes supporting their children. Attend their children's events, celebrate their achievements, and offer help when needed. This support creates a sense of extended family and reinforces the values of community and compassion. We make an effort to attend each other's children's sports games, recitals, and other events, showing our support and building a sense of community.

Create opportunities for mutual support. Life's challenges are easier to face with a supportive network. Offer and seek support from other families during difficult times. This could include providing meals, helping with childcare, or simply being there to listen and offer encouragement. In our community, we have a support group that organizes meal deliveries and assistance for families going through tough times, creating a strong network of care.

By building relationships with other families, you create a supportive and nurturing network that enhances your spiritual journey. These connections provide friendship, mutual support, and opportunities for shared growth. Embracing these relationships enriches your family's faith experience and fosters a sense of extended family within your faith community.

## Serving Together as a Family

Serving together as a family is like strengthening the foundation of your family house. It reinforces your values, deepens your bonds, and provides a sense of purpose. When we began serving together, it transformed our family dynamics and brought us closer. Let's explore how you can serve together as a family and make a positive impact while enriching your spiritual journey.

Identify causes that resonate with your family. Start by discussing the issues and causes that are important to each family member. Look for common interests and passions. Whether it's helping the homeless, supporting the environment, or advocating for social justice, finding a cause that resonates with everyone makes the experience more meaningful. In our family, we all share a passion for helping the less fortunate, so we often focus our efforts on local shelters and food banks.

Find family-friendly volunteer opportunities. Look for volunteer activities that are suitable for all ages and that you can do together. Many organizations offer family-friendly volunteer opportunities, such as serving meals at a shelter, participating in community clean-ups, or organizing donation drives. Choose activities that align with your family's interests and availability. We found that volunteering at a local food bank was a great way for all of us to contribute, regardless of age.

Incorporate service into your routine. Make serving others a regular part of your family's life, rather than a one-time event. Schedule regular volunteer activities, such as monthly visits to a nursing home or weekly community clean-ups. Consistency reinforces the importance of service and makes it a natural part of your routine. We set aside one Saturday each month for a family service project, which has become a cherished tradition.

Reflect on your experiences together. After each service activity, take time to reflect on your experiences as a family. Discuss what you learned, how it made you feel, and how it aligns with your faith and values. This reflection deepens your understanding and reinforces the significance of your efforts. After volunteering, we often have a family discussion over dinner, sharing our thoughts and feelings about the experience.

Use your talents and skills. Each family member has unique talents and skills that can be used to serve others. Identify these strengths and find ways to apply them in your volunteer activities. Whether it's cooking, organizing, teaching, or crafting, using your skills makes your contributions more impactful and enjoyable. For instance, our daughter loves baking, so we often bake cookies together to donate to local shelters.

Involve your faith community. Serving together as a family can inspire others in your faith community to join in. Share your experiences and invite other families to participate in your service activities. This not only amplifies your impact but also builds a stronger sense of community. We often invite other families from our church to join us in our volunteer projects, creating a larger, more powerful force for good.

Celebrate your contributions. Recognize and celebrate the efforts and achievements of your family's service. This could be through a special meal, a thank-you note, or simply acknowledging each person's contributions. Celebrating your service reinforces its importance and encourages continued involvement. After completing a major project, we always celebrate with a special family outing or treat, acknowledging everyone's hard work and dedication.

By serving together as a family, you strengthen your bonds, reinforce your values, and make a positive impact on your community. These activities not only enrich your spiritual journey but also provide a sense of purpose and fulfillment.

# Creating Inclusive and Welcoming Spaces

Creating inclusive and welcoming spaces within your faith community is like opening the doors of your family house to everyone. It's about fostering an environment where everyone feels valued, respected, and part of the family. When we focused on making our faith community more inclusive, we saw a remarkable transformation in how people connected and supported each other. Let's explore how you can create these inclusive and welcoming spaces.

Start by promoting a culture of respect and acceptance. Encourage your family and faith community to embrace diversity in all its forms, including different backgrounds, beliefs, abilities, and perspectives. Foster an environment where everyone feels heard and valued. This culture of respect and acceptance begins with small actions, like greeting newcomers warmly and being open to different viewpoints. In our faith community, we make it a point to welcome new members personally and invite them to join in activities.

Ensure accessibility for all. Make sure that your faith community's physical spaces are accessible to everyone, including those with disabilities. This might involve installing ramps, providing hearing assistance devices, or creating sensory-friendly areas. Accessibility goes beyond physical spaces; consider how you can make your programs and activities inclusive as well. For example, our church recently installed wheelchair ramps and made our services available online for those who can't attend in person.

Offer diverse programming. Plan events and activities that cater to a wide range of interests and needs. This could include different types of worship services, educational programs, and social events. Offering a variety of programs ensures that everyone can find something that resonates with them and helps them feel included. We've found that having a mix of traditional and contemporary services, as well as educational workshops, appeals to a broader audience.

Encourage active participation. Create opportunities for everyone to get involved and contribute their talents and skills. This could be through volunteer roles, leadership positions, or participating in planning committees. Encouraging active participation helps people feel invested and valued in the community. We actively invite members to lead prayers, join committees, and share their skills in various church activities, fostering a sense of ownership and involvement.

Provide support and resources. Be proactive in identifying and addressing the needs of your community members. This could involve offering counseling services, support groups, or financial assistance programs. Providing support and resources helps create a caring and responsive community. For example, we started a support group for parents of children with special needs, offering them a safe space to share experiences and find resources.

Celebrate cultural and spiritual diversity. Recognize and celebrate the diverse backgrounds and traditions within your faith community. This could involve hosting cultural events, celebrating different religious holidays, or incorporating diverse traditions into your services. Celebrating diversity enriches your community and fosters a deeper understanding and appreciation of each other. We host an annual cultural festival where members can share their heritage through food, music, and storytelling.

By creating inclusive and welcoming spaces, you foster a sense of belonging and community. These practices ensure that everyone feels valued and respected, enriching your faith community and strengthening its bonds. Embracing inclusivity and welcome enhances your family's spiritual journey and creates a vibrant, supportive environment for all.

## Strengthening Intergenerational Connections

Strengthening intergenerational connections within your faith community is like weaving a tapestry that includes threads from every age group. These connections enrich everyone's spiritual journey and build a stronger, more cohesive community. When we began focusing on intergenerational relationships, it brought new perspectives and deeper bonds within our community. Let's explore how you can strengthen these connections.

Encourage mentorship and sharing of wisdom. Create opportunities for older members to mentor younger ones, sharing their experiences, wisdom, and faith journey. This could involve formal mentorship programs, storytelling sessions, or simply fostering natural relationships. Mentorship helps bridge the gap between generations and provides valuable guidance. In our church, we paired seniors with youth in a mentorship program that has fostered meaningful connections and mutual growth.

Organize intergenerational activities. Plan events and activities that bring different age groups together. This could include family game nights, community service projects, or intergenerational worship services. These activities create opportunities for interaction, learning, and bonding. We've found that organizing community service projects where all ages can participate helps build strong, cross-generational relationships.

Create spaces for dialogue and collaboration. Provide forums where different generations can come together to discuss their perspectives, share their stories, and collaborate on projects. This could be through discussion groups, workshops, or joint planning committees. These spaces promote understanding and respect between generations. We established an intergenerational discussion group that meets monthly to talk about various topics, fostering open dialogue and mutual respect.

Celebrate milestones together. Recognize and celebrate the important milestones in the lives of your community members, such as birthdays, anniversaries, graduations, and retirements. Celebrating these events together strengthens the sense of community and acknowledges the contributions of each generation. Our church holds monthly celebrations where we honor significant milestones, bringing everyone together to celebrate and support each other.

Encourage learning from each other. Promote a culture of continuous learning where all generations can teach and learn from each other. This could involve skill-sharing workshops, joint educational programs, or collaborative projects. Learning from each other enriches everyone's experience and fosters mutual respect. We organized skill-sharing workshops where older members taught traditional crafts, and younger members shared their expertise in technology, creating a valuable exchange of knowledge.

Support family involvement. Encourage families to participate in community activities together, reinforcing the importance of family bonds and intergenerational connections. Family-oriented events and programs help create a supportive environment where everyone feels included. We introduced family-friendly service projects that allow all ages to work together, fostering stronger family and community ties.

By strengthening intergenerational connections, you create a rich, supportive tapestry of relationships within your faith community. These practices foster mutual respect, learning, and understanding, enriching everyone's spiritual journey. Embracing intergenerational connections enhances your family's experience and creates a vibrant, cohesive community for all.

## Fostering a Spirit of Generosity

Fostering a spirit of generosity within your family and faith community is like opening the windows of your family house to let in fresh, invigorating air. Generosity enriches both the giver and the receiver, creating a culture of kindness and abundance. When we focused on fostering generosity, it transformed our interactions and strengthened our community. Let's explore how you can cultivate a spirit of generosity.

Start by modeling generosity. Demonstrate generous behavior in your own actions, whether it's through giving your time, resources, or support. Your example sets a powerful precedent for your family and community. Share stories of generosity and its impact, inspiring others to follow suit. In our family, we make it a point to share our experiences of giving and the joy it brings, reinforcing the value of generosity.

Encourage regular acts of kindness. Make generosity a regular part of your family's routine by encouraging small, everyday acts of kindness. This could be helping a neighbor, volunteering, or simply offering a kind word. These acts build a habit of giving and show that generosity doesn't always require grand gestures. We started a "kindness calendar" where each day we perform a small act of kindness, fostering a habit of generosity.

Teach the value of giving. Educate your family, especially children, about the importance and impact of generosity. Discuss how giving can make a difference in someone's life and how it aligns with your faith and values. Use stories, examples, and hands-on activities to illustrate these lessons. We often read stories about generosity and discuss them, helping our children understand the significance of giving.

Create opportunities for giving. Provide practical ways for your family and community to practice generosity. This could include donation drives, fundraising events, or volunteer opportunities. Having concrete opportunities to give makes it easier for people to participate and see the impact of their generosity. We organize regular donation drives and community service projects, making it easy for everyone to get involved.

Celebrate and acknowledge generosity. Recognize and celebrate acts of generosity within your family and community. This acknowledgment reinforces the value of giving and encourages continued generosity. Whether it's a simple thank-you note, a public acknowledgment, or a small celebration, showing appreciation goes a long way. We created a "generosity wall" in our church where we post stories and acknowledgments of generous acts, celebrating and inspiring others.

Foster a mindset of abundance. Teach your family to view the world through a lens of abundance rather than scarcity. This mindset shift encourages giving, as it focuses on what you have to offer rather than what you lack. Practice gratitude and emphasize the blessings in your life, reinforcing the idea that there is always enough to share. We regularly practice gratitude as a family, reflecting on our blessings and how we can share them with others.

By fostering a spirit of generosity, you create a culture of kindness, abundance, and mutual support. These practices enrich your family and community, strengthening bonds and creating a positive, uplifting environment. Embracing generosity enhances your spiritual journey and builds a more compassionate, connected faith community.

# Chapter 9
## Leaving a Lasting Legacy

### Documenting Your Family's Story

Documenting your family's story is like creating a detailed blueprint of your family house that future generations can reference and cherish. When we began to document our family's history, it not only preserved our memories but also deepened our sense of identity and connection. Let's explore how you can document your family's story and create a lasting legacy.

Start by gathering stories and memories. Collect stories from different family members, focusing on significant events, traditions, and personal experiences. These stories can provide a rich tapestry of your family's history and values. Encourage each person to share their memories, whether through interviews, written accounts, or voice recordings. In our family, we held a series of "storytelling nights" where each person shared their favorite family memories, which we recorded for posterity.

Create a family history book. Compile the stories, photos, and documents into a beautifully crafted family history book. This book can include timelines, family trees, and personal anecdotes, providing a comprehensive record of your family's journey. You can use online tools or professional services to create a polished and durable book. We created a family history book that includes photos, handwritten letters, and even old recipes, capturing the essence of our family's past.

Incorporate multimedia elements. Use modern technology to enrich your documentation process. Create digital archives that include video interviews, audio recordings, and scanned documents. These multimedia elements can bring your family's history to life in a dynamic and engaging way. We started a digital family archive, uploading videos of family gatherings, voice recordings of stories, and digital copies of important documents, ensuring that these memories are preserved and accessible.

Highlight values and lessons. Ensure that your documentation reflects not just the events, but also the values and lessons that have shaped your family. Include reflections on how faith, resilience, and love have guided your family through various challenges and triumphs. This focus on values ensures that your legacy is more than just a record of events; it's a guide for future generations. In our family history book, we included sections where each member shared their thoughts on the values they hold dear and the lessons they've learned.

Regularly update your documentation. Family history is always evolving, so make it a habit to update your records regularly. Add new stories, photos, and milestones as they happen. This ongoing documentation keeps your family's story current and ensures that no significant events are forgotten. We set aside time each year to update our family history book and digital archive, adding new memories and reflecting on the past year.

Share your family's story. Make your documentation accessible to all family members, ensuring that everyone can learn from and appreciate your shared history. Consider creating multiple copies of your family history book or providing digital access to your archives. Sharing your family's story strengthens connections and ensures that the legacy is passed down through generations. We gifted each family member a copy of our family history book during a special gathering, reinforcing our shared heritage and values.

By documenting your family's story, you create a lasting legacy that future generations can cherish and learn from. These practices preserve your memories, highlight your values, and strengthen your family's identity and connections. Embracing the process of documenting your family's history enriches your spiritual journey and ensures that your legacy endures.

## Passing Down Traditions and Values

Passing down traditions and values is like embedding strong pillars into your family house, ensuring stability and continuity for generations to come. When we focused on transmitting our traditions and values, it created a strong foundation for our family's future. Let's explore how you can effectively pass down your family's traditions and values.

Start by identifying key traditions and values. Reflect on the traditions and values that are most important to your family. These might include holiday celebrations, religious practices, cultural customs, or core principles like honesty, compassion, and perseverance. Make a list of these traditions and values, and discuss their significance with your family. In our family, we identified key traditions such as our holiday rituals and core values like kindness and integrity.

Involve all generations. Engage family members of all ages in practicing and discussing your traditions and values. Encourage older members to share their experiences and stories, and involve younger ones in the activities and discussions. This intergenerational involvement reinforces the continuity and importance of these traditions and values. We often invite grandparents to share stories and lead activities during family gatherings, ensuring that their wisdom and experiences are passed down.

Create meaningful rituals. Establish rituals that embody your family's values and traditions. These could be daily, weekly, or annual practices that bring your family together and reinforce your shared beliefs. Rituals provide structure and meaning, making traditions and values a living part of your family life. For example, we have a weekly family dinner where we not only share a meal but also discuss our week and reflect on our values.

Celebrate your traditions. Make an effort to celebrate and honor your family's traditions regularly. These celebrations can be small or large, but they should always be meaningful and reflective of your values. Use these occasions to teach and remind family members of the importance of these traditions. During our holiday celebrations, we always take time to explain the significance of each tradition and how it connects to our values.

Document and share your traditions and values. Create a written or digital record of your family's traditions and values. This documentation can include descriptions of each tradition, its origins, and the values it represents. Share this record with all family members, ensuring that the knowledge is preserved and accessible. We created a family traditions and values book, which we update regularly and share with all family members, providing a tangible record of our heritage.

Adapt and evolve. Be open to adapting your traditions and values to fit the changing dynamics of your family. While it's important to preserve your heritage, allowing room for evolution ensures that your traditions remain relevant and meaningful. Encourage input from all family members on how to keep traditions alive in ways that resonate with everyone. We regularly discuss how we can adapt our traditions to fit our current circumstances while still honoring their core essence.

By passing down traditions and values, you create a strong foundation for your family's legacy. These practices ensure that your heritage is preserved and that future generations understand and appreciate the principles that guide your family. Embracing the process of transmitting traditions and values enriches your spiritual journey and strengthens your family's bonds.

## Planning for the Future

Planning for the future is like drawing up blueprints for the extensions and improvements of your family house, ensuring its growth and sustainability. When we began to take intentional steps to plan for our family's future, it provided clarity, direction, and peace of mind. Let's explore how you can effectively plan for your family's future and create a lasting legacy.

Start with clear goals and objectives. Identify the long-term goals and objectives for your family. These might include financial stability, educational achievements, spiritual growth, or specific family projects. Having clear goals provides direction and helps you focus your efforts. In our family, we set goals for financial security, educational milestones for our children, and plans for family vacations and gatherings.

Create a comprehensive financial plan. Financial planning is crucial for securing your family's future. This includes budgeting, saving, investing, and planning for major expenses like education and retirement. Consider working with a financial advisor to create a robust financial plan that aligns with your family's goals. We worked with a financial advisor to create a plan that includes savings for our children's education, retirement accounts, and investments for future security.

Develop an estate plan. An estate plan ensures that your assets are distributed according to your wishes and that your family is taken care of in the event of your passing. This includes creating a will, setting up trusts, and designating beneficiaries. Regularly review and update your estate plan to reflect any changes in your family's circumstances. We set up a family trust and created wills to ensure our assets are managed and distributed as we intend.

Invest in education and personal development. Plan for the educational and personal development needs of your family members. This might include saving for college, supporting ongoing education, or investing in personal growth opportunities. Encourage lifelong learning and provide resources to help family members achieve their educational goals. We set up education savings accounts for our children and support them in pursuing additional learning opportunities.

Prepare for unforeseen events. Life is unpredictable, and it's important to have contingency plans in place. This includes having adequate insurance coverage (health, life, disability), setting up emergency funds, and creating plans for unexpected events like job loss or medical emergencies. Preparing for the unexpected provides peace of mind and ensures that your family can navigate challenges with resilience. We reviewed our insurance policies and built an emergency fund to cover potential unexpected expenses.

Encourage open communication and planning discussions. Regularly discuss your family's future plans and goals with all members. Encourage everyone to share their thoughts, aspirations, and concerns. Open communication ensures that everyone is aligned and invested in the family's future. We hold family meetings every few months to discuss our progress towards goals, address any concerns, and plan for upcoming events or changes.

By planning for the future, you ensure that your family is prepared for whatever lies ahead. These practices provide direction, security, and peace of mind, creating a strong foundation for your family's legacy. Embracing the process of future planning enriches your spiritual journey and strengthens your family's bonds, ensuring that your legacy endures.

# Creating a Legacy of Service

Creating a legacy of service is like planting a garden that will continue to flourish and provide for others long after you are gone. When we committed to service as a cornerstone of our family legacy, it not only enriched our lives but also made a positive impact on our community. Let's explore how you can build a lasting legacy of service.

Identify causes you're passionate about. Start by discussing with your family the causes and issues that matter most to you. Whether it's education, healthcare, environmental conservation, or social justice, finding a shared passion makes your efforts more meaningful and focused. In our family, we discovered a shared passion for supporting local education initiatives, which became a central part of our service legacy.

Integrate service into your family's routine. Make service a regular part of your family's life by scheduling volunteer activities and community service projects. Whether it's monthly visits to a local shelter, annual participation in charity events, or weekly contributions to a food bank, consistency is key. Regular involvement reinforces the importance of service and makes it a natural part of your family's identity. We made it a tradition to volunteer at our local food bank every first Saturday of the month, which has become a cherished family activity.

Encourage each family member to contribute. Recognize that everyone has unique talents and interests that can be used in service. Encourage each family member to find their own way to contribute, whether through hands-on volunteering, fundraising, advocacy, or creative projects. This individual involvement fosters a sense of ownership and personal commitment to service. Our children, for example, started a school supplies drive, using their organizational skills and creativity to support underprivileged students.

Partner with local organizations. Collaborate with community organizations, nonprofits, and faith-based groups that align with your family's service goals. These partnerships can amplify your impact and provide additional resources and support. Building strong relationships with local organizations also helps you stay connected to the community and understand its needs better. We partnered with a local nonprofit focused on literacy, supporting their programs through volunteer work and donations.

Document and celebrate your service. Keep a record of your family's service activities, including photos, reflections, and outcomes. This documentation not only preserves memories but also highlights the impact of your efforts. Celebrate your achievements and milestones together, acknowledging the difference you've made. We created a family service scrapbook, where we document our projects and reflect on the positive changes we've contributed to, celebrating our journey of service.

Pass on the value of service to future generations. Ensure that the importance of service is communicated and instilled in younger family members. Share stories of your family's service history and involve children in volunteer activities from a young age. Teaching the next generation about the value of giving back ensures that your legacy of service continues. We often talk about the impact of service at family gatherings, encouraging our children to carry on the tradition of helping others.

By creating a legacy of service, you make a lasting positive impact on your community and instill valuable principles in your family. These practices enrich your lives, strengthen your bonds, and ensure that your legacy of kindness and compassion endures for generations to come.

## Cultivating Lifelong Learning

Cultivating a love for lifelong learning within your family is like building a library in your family house—an endless source of knowledge, growth, and inspiration. When we prioritized education and continuous learning, it opened doors to new opportunities and enriched our lives profoundly. Let's explore how you can foster a culture of lifelong learning in your family.

Encourage curiosity and exploration. Foster an environment where asking questions, seeking answers, and exploring new interests are encouraged. Provide resources such as books, documentaries, and educational games that stimulate curiosity. Celebrate the joy of discovery and learning together. In our family, we have a weekly "discovery night" where we explore a new topic or activity, from science experiments to cultural studies.

Set aside dedicated learning time. Create a routine that includes time for reading, studying, and pursuing educational interests. This could be a quiet reading hour, a family study session, or an online course everyone takes together. Having a regular time dedicated to learning reinforces its importance and makes it a consistent part of your lives. We established a nightly reading hour where each family member reads a book of their choice, followed by a short discussion about what we learned.

Lead by example. Demonstrate your commitment to lifelong learning by pursuing your own educational interests and goals. Share your experiences and the joy you find in learning new things. Your enthusiasm and dedication will inspire other family members to value and pursue their own learning journeys. I often share my experiences from the courses I'm taking and discuss the interesting insights I've gained, which motivates my family to explore their own educational paths.

Use technology to enhance learning. Take advantage of the vast array of online resources available for learning. This includes educational websites, online courses, virtual museum tours, and language learning apps. Integrating technology into your learning activities can make education more accessible and engaging. We subscribed to several online learning platforms that offer courses on a wide range of subjects, allowing each of us to explore our interests at our own pace.

Create a learning-friendly environment. Designate spaces in your home that are conducive to studying and learning. These spaces should be quiet, comfortable, and equipped with the necessary resources such as books, computers, and art supplies. A dedicated learning space helps minimize distractions and fosters a focused, productive atmosphere. We set up a home library and study nook, complete with comfortable seating and plenty of educational materials.

Celebrate educational achievements. Recognize and celebrate milestones and accomplishments in your learning journeys. This could include finishing a book, completing a course, or mastering a new skill. Celebrating achievements reinforces the value of learning and motivates continued efforts. We hold a monthly "achievement celebration" where we acknowledge each family member's educational milestones, no matter how big or small.

Encourage collaborative learning. Engage in learning activities together as a family. This could include group projects, educational games, or family outings to museums and cultural events. Collaborative learning strengthens family bonds and makes education a shared and enjoyable experience. We often visit museums, attend educational workshops, and play trivia games together, making learning a fun and collective endeavor.

By cultivating lifelong learning, you create a dynamic and intellectually stimulating environment for your family. These practices encourage curiosity, growth, and continuous improvement, enriching your lives and strengthening your family's legacy of knowledge and education. Embracing lifelong learning enhances your spiritual journey and ensures that your family remains curious, informed, and inspired.

## Nurturing Spiritual Growth

Nurturing spiritual growth within your family is like tending to a garden that will continue to bloom and thrive. When we focused on nurturing our spiritual growth, it deepened our faith and brought us closer together. Let's explore how you can foster spiritual growth in your family, creating a strong foundation of faith and connection.

Create regular spiritual practices. Establish daily or weekly routines that include spiritual activities such as prayer, meditation, scripture reading, and attending worship services. Consistent spiritual practices provide a framework for growth and help keep your family connected to their faith. In our family, we have a nightly prayer and reflection time, where we come together to pray and discuss our spiritual insights.

Encourage personal spiritual exploration. Support each family member in exploring their own spiritual path and practices. This might include journaling, attending retreats, or studying different aspects of your faith. Providing space for personal spiritual exploration fosters a deeper, more personal connection to faith. We encourage our children to keep spiritual journals where they write down their thoughts, prayers, and reflections, and we periodically discuss their insights.

Engage in family discussions about faith. Create an open and supportive environment where family members can discuss their beliefs, doubts, and spiritual experiences. These discussions can deepen understanding and provide mutual support on your spiritual journeys. We have regular family discussions where we talk about our faith, share our experiences, and address any questions or concerns, fostering a deeper collective understanding.

Participate in community service. Serving others is a powerful way to live out your faith and nurture spiritual growth. Engage in service projects as a family, helping those in need and making a positive impact in your community. Reflect on these experiences and their spiritual significance. We regularly volunteer at a local shelter, finding that these acts of service not only help others but also strengthen our own faith and sense of purpose.

Explore different spiritual resources. Utilize a variety of resources to support your family's spiritual growth. This could include books, podcasts, online sermons, and spiritual workshops. Exploring different resources provides fresh perspectives and insights that can enhance your spiritual journey. We subscribed to several faith-based podcasts and online sermon series, which we listen to and discuss as a family.

Model spiritual growth. Demonstrate your commitment to spiritual growth through your actions and attitudes. Share your spiritual practices and experiences with your family, showing them the importance of continual growth and reflection. Your example can inspire and motivate others to pursue their own spiritual development. I often share my own spiritual practices and the insights I gain, encouraging my family to reflect on their own journeys.

Celebrate spiritual milestones. Recognize and celebrate significant spiritual milestones and achievements within your family. This could include baptisms, confirmations, or personal spiritual breakthroughs. Celebrating these moments reinforces their importance and encourages continued growth. We hold special family gatherings to celebrate spiritual milestones, such as our children's confirmations, making these occasions memorable and meaningful.

By nurturing spiritual growth, you create a strong foundation of faith and connection within your family. These practices foster a deeper understanding of your beliefs, strengthen your spiritual bonds, and support each person's individual journey. Embracing spiritual growth enriches your family's legacy and ensures that your faith continues to thrive and inspire future generations.

Made in the USA
Columbia, SC
08 February 2025

52880612R00080